Praise for *Dogs and the Wo*

"Whether you're a 'normal' dog mo̲m̲, ̲o̲ ̲p̲s̲y̲c̲h̲o̲ ̲dog mom…or somewhere in between, this book will open your heart, warm your soul, and make you proud to be a dog-loving woman."
— from the foreword by Rory Freedman,
coauthor of *Skinny Bitch*

"Perhaps because my older sister was a collie, I am never more myself than when in the presence of a dog. Kudos to Allen and Linda for sharing the myriad ways dogs bring joy, healing, and gratitude into our lives."
— Wendie Malick, actor and advocate

"Once again the Andersons have produced an inspiring book for women who love dogs, this time packed with stories and meditations that will make you smile, weep, and be moved by scenes ranging from Katrina rescues to a dog dazzling David Letterman on his *Late Night* show. If you have a special relationship with your dogs, this book is for you."
— Linda Tellington-Jones, PhD (Hon), founder of the
Tellington TTouch Method® and author of
Getting in TTouch with Your Dog

"Cuddle up with your dog and prepare to be profoundly moved by these heartwarming stories of the special bond that exists between women and their dogs. In reading each story, you will be humbled by the virtuous characteristics of our dog companions who clearly cherish sharing their lives with us. These powerful stories will resonate deeply with anyone who has ever loved a dog."
— June Cotner, author of *Animal Blessings* and *Dog Blessings*

"This charming collection of true stories will affirm people's feelings about the love and spiritual nature of our wonderful canine companions."
— Sonya Fitzpatrick, television and radio host and author of *What the Animals Tell Me*

Praise for Allen and Linda Anderson's books

"Reading *Angel Dogs* is like taking a walk in the park on a sunny day with your favorite dog."
— Willard Scott, NBC's *Today* show

"My heart was touched by *Angel Cats*. Read, laugh, cry, and become a more complete human being through the angel cats and the lifeline they provide."
— Bernie Siegel, MD, author of *365 Prescriptions for the Soul* and *Love, Medicine & Miracles*

"Angels come to us in many ways. Some are never identified; some come to us and we don't even know they changed our lives, maybe even saved us, until there is a realization. This book is enlightening and will make you take many a close look at your 'angel.'"
— Tippi Hedren, actress and animal activist

"All traditional peoples have viewed animals as messengers and mediators of the divine, which is a lesson we need to relearn. *Angel Animals Book of Inspiration* is a bold reminder that consciousness takes many forms and is not restricted to humans."
— Larry Dossey, MD, author of *Healing beyond the Body* and *Healing Words*

DOGS
and the Women
Who Love Them

Also by Allen and Linda Anderson

Angel Animals: Divine Messengers of Miracles

Angel Animals Book of Inspiration:
Divine Messengers of Wisdom and Compassion

Angel Cats: Divine Messengers of Comfort

Angel Dogs: Divine Messengers of Love

Angel Dogs with a Mission:
Divine Messengers in Service to All Life

Angel Horses: Divine Messengers of Hope

Horses with a Mission:
Extraordinary True Stories of Equine Service

Rainbows and Bridges: An Animal Companion Memorial Kit

Rescued: Saving Animals from Disaster

Saying Goodbye to Your Angel Animals:
Finding Comfort After Losing Your Pet

DOGS
and the Women Who Love Them

Extraordinary True Stories of Loyalty,
Healing, and Inspiration

Allen and Linda Anderson

Foreword by Rory Freedman

New World Library
Novato, California

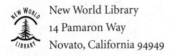

New World Library
14 Pamaron Way
Novato, California 94949

Angel Animals® is a registered trademark of Allen and Linda Anderson
TTouch® is a registered trademark of Linda Tellington-Jones

Text design by Tona Pearce Myers

Library of Congress Cataloging-in-Publication Data
Anderson, Allen, date.
 Dogs and the women who love them : extraordinary true stories of loyalty, healing, and inspiration / Allen and Linda Anderson ; foreword by Rory Freedman.
    p. cm.
Includes bibliographical references.
ISBN 978-1-57731-692-3 (pbk. : alk. paper)
1. Women dog owners—United States—Anecdotes. 2. Human-animal relationships—United States—Anecdotes. I. Anderson, Linda C., date. II. Title.
SF422.7.A63 2010
636.70092'9—dc22   2010029976

First printing, October 2010
ISBN 978-1-57731-692-3

Printed in Canada on 100% postconsumer-waste recycled paper

 New World Library is a proud member of the Green Press Initiative.

10 9 8 7 6 5 4 3 2 1

Contents

Three. Embracing Life

Foreword

I'm not trying to be witty or funny when I say: I think I was a dog in a past life. That, or I'm totally in touch with my primal side. Because I don't just kiss and hug and squeeze my dogs — I also bite them. A lot. I love them so much it makes me feel a little sick. Heady too. I love their furry little bodies, the smell of their paws (corn chips and grass), and all the ridiculously funny things they do. Every morning, when Joey, my black Lab, yawns, she sounds like a Wookiee. And I recently caught Timber, my yellow Lab, tiptoeing. Tiptoeing — I swear! I wanted him out of the kitchen, so I told him to go outside and play. He left, begrudgingly, and I carried on cooking. A minute or two later, I heard the light clickety-clack of his nails on the floor. I turned around and saw him tiptoeing, all stealthy, trying to sneak back in undetected.

I have an unusual situation in that my dogs live with me, in Los Angeles, for only six months out of the year. (They spend the other six months with their dad in Lake Tahoe. I know it sounds strange to some people, but yes, my ex-boyfriend and I share custody of our dogs. We adopted them together and both love them, so why wouldn't we both still take care of them? He and I are on great terms, and his sweet girlfriend is a second mom to the dogs and loves them as much as we do.) So maybe my crazy, obsessive love for my dogs is a result of having to squeeze it all into half a year, but probably not. I see full-time dog moms who are equally obsessed with their dogs.

In *Dogs and the Women Who Love Them*, I have met such kindred spirits. Teresa Ambord brought as much love and warmth to a senior center as her dog Sandy did, inciting much of the same in return. Rosanne Nordstrom opened her heart to beloved Newfoundland Miguel, changing the course of her life in a most unexpected way. And renowned author and animal activist Karen Dawn so beautifully reflects on her relationship with soul mate Buster Dawn, and on surviving profound loss.

My two little muppets are unbridled love and joy; I can hardly imagine they will one day be gone. That they love me so uncondi-

Rory with Joey (left) and Timber

tionally is such a gift, one I sometimes feel unworthy of. Not that they're at all discerning, but I'd like to be a mom they'd be proud of. So I'm thankful that Timber and Joey inspire me to continue my work as an animal rights activist. Whenever I look in their soulful eyes, I am reminded of all the animals in zoos, circuses, rodeos, labs, and slaughterhouses. And I know that all animals are one and the same, and that I must work to end their pain and suffering. The day I learned how cows, chickens, and pigs become meat was a day my life changed. Becoming vegetarian and then eventually vegan were the two best decisions I've ever made. I couldn't continue to call myself an animal lover and contribute to the torture and slaughter of animals just because I liked how they tasted. Every time Timber and Joey enjoy a hike, a treat, or a loving touch, I'm reminded of the billions of animals who are suffering and that I must be a voice for them.

My dogs have taught me so much — patience, unconditional love, and, of course, compassion. Additionally, they always remind me of the secret to happiness. Whether we're all cuddling on the couch watching a movie or hiking on a beautiful trail, they are fully present. They rejoice at everything — being with the ones they love, the same landscape they've seen a hundred times, or catching some scent in the air. I am constantly learning from them to slow down, be appreciative, and enjoy things exactly as they are. And in some cases, they remind me to change things that don't suit my needs. When Timber gets into my bed, he kicks at the blankets and pillows, moving everything around until it's just right. When other dogs come up to Joey and she's not in the mood to socialize, she'll bark, snarl, and growl until they leave her alone. My mission in life is to make the world a better place for animals, so until things change — until people change — I too am going to kick up the covers and bark, snarl, and growl.

Whether you're a "normal" dog mom, a psycho dog mom (you love so deeply, you bite), or somewhere in between, this book will open your heart, warm your soul, and make you proud to be a dog-loving woman.

— Rory Freedman, psycho dog mom, vegan,
animal rights activist, and coauthor of the
#1 *New York Times* bestseller *Skinny Bitch*,
Skinny Bitch in the Kitch, *Skinny Bitch: Bun in the Oven*,
Skinny Bitchin', and *Skinny Bastard* (www.skinnybitch.net)

Introduction

I am so small I can barely be seen.
How can this great love be inside me?

Look at your eyes. They are small,
but they see enormous things.

—JALAL AL-DIN RUMI (1207–1273), "The Turn: Dance in Your Blood"

Walking in rhythm to each other's steps, enjoying the warmth of a spring day, senses keen and alert, a woman and her dog team up to take on the world. The unique bond between women and their best furry friends fascinates us with its simple purity and shared unconditional love. This book explores one of the most compelling and devoted interspecies relationships on the planet — the one that exists between dogs and women. The women who share their stories in these pages have discovered that relating to a special dog unlocks countless doors to inner strength, self-discovery, spiritual growth, comfort, health, and fulfillment.

This book is about the change that occurs when dogs and women transform each other's lives by offering expanded viewpoints of what is possible. It introduces dogs who have learned that in spite of their previous abuse and abandonment, they can trust some humans again.

Dogs and the women who love them bring out the best in each other, because women transcend what is *humanly* achievable when they forge authentic bonds with canine companions.

As women, with their nurturing natures, join with dogs, who are loyal and affectionate, they form strong teams that plow through obstacles and perform courageous acts of kindness and compassion. These remarkable women and their amazing dogs light pathways on which all of us can explore our higher natures.

The stories reveal the subtle beauty and effectiveness of silent inner channels of communication between species. As dogs listen — by paying attention — to women, and as women listen to dogs, they acquire wisdom that is too sweet for words, too exquisite for explanation. Dogs and the women who love them exchange glances and understand each other without speaking. They curl up together and luxuriate in the warm touch of skin against fur. Unlike most human pairs, who require ongoing conversations for interaction, a woman and a dog become soul mates without the dog ever saying a word.

Women and dogs dance in harmony with life. As long as they are partners, it doesn't matter if the dance turns gentle, stormy, joyous, or heartbreaking. They take turns leading and following. They adapt. Simply put, they *get* each other.

How Women and Dogs Got Together

Jon Franklin, a Pulitzer Prize–winning science journalist, presents a fascinating theory about the symbiotic origin of dog-human relationships. In *The Wolf in the Parlor*, Franklin presents a plausible theory of human-dog evolution. He says that about twelve thousand years ago, wild wolves evolved into follower wolves and hung around human camps to catch scraps of food. After the follower wolves became domesticated, a mutually beneficial relationship developed that literally changed the brain structures of dogs and humans.[1]

Franklin says that, about the same time in history, dogs and humans both had a reduction in brain mass. He theorizes that, in a mutually beneficial trade-off, they took over tasks and functions for each other. "We [humans] hadn't actually lost that brain matter; we had just handed it to the dog to carry. The dog was more than guard and hunting companion. It was our beast of emotional burden.... The dog was keeper of the deep emotional past. It was our emotional guide dog. Emotion was as clearly the dog's specialty, as thought was ours."[2]

According to Franklin, dogs became our best friends when they took on the primal function of surrogate for our emotions. He claims that it's not so much that the puppy steals our heart as that a dog functions as a missing piece of the human brain's limbic system, the seat of emotions.[3]

Since ancient times, women and dogs have related to each other at a deeply emotional level. Franklin writes, "Thirty to forty thousand years ago, in the case of the wolf, even a brief stay with humans was a step toward domestication, and a big one.... My growing suspicion [is] that women, not men, were the primary force in the appearance of the dog."[4] He theorizes that Paleolithic females were responsible for allowing friendly wolf cubs to live with human families and even play with their children until the cubs grew into adulthood and their wild wolf nature emerged.[5]

But how did our relationship with dogs grow into one that involves our reliance on them for more than carrying human emotional baggage? In today's human-dog interactions, dogs, with their social intelligence, take on the role of protector. And women, especially, appreciate these canine security systems.

"The Secrets Inside Your Dog's Mind," by Carl Zimmer, offers a theory about a dog's valuable ability and instinct to keep intruders away from his cave or from attacking his pack. "Once dogs became comfortable in our company, humans began to speed up dogs' social evolution. They may have started by giving extra food to helpful dogs — ones that barked to warn of danger, say. Dogs that paid close attention to humans got rewards and eventually became partners with humans, helping with hunts or herding other animals. Along the way, the dogs' social intelligence became eerily like ours."[6]

The combination of canine social intelligence and emotional resonance makes women value a dog's opinion about potential love interests. It also makes many women prefer the company of their dogs to that of their spouses.

Love Me, Love My Dog

A 2005 BizRate Research study of 901 people with pets revealed that over 50 percent of the women respondents considered their pets to be a stronger source of love and affection than their marriage partners. Over 70 percent of the women with pets said they would be more likely to date or marry a man who has a pet.[7] Also, in *Women Want More*, Michael J. Silverstein, Kate Sayre, and John Butman report an astonishing finding: the Boston Consulting Group Global Inquiry into Women and Consumerism, a 2008 survey of twelve thousand women from all walks of life in twenty-two countries, revealed that pets make women happier than having sex.[8]

We did some informal research by asking a question on Twitter and Facebook to see what our friends and fans had to say about the subject of dogs and men. We posted: "Has a dog helped you find or keep a good man? Ladies, tell us your stories." As you can imagine, we received a wide range and large number of interesting responses. With their permission we're retelling some of the stories that the women emailed to us.

First there were the women who had experiences with dogs as heart-alerts and protectors. The consensus was that dogs instinctively read the emotional states of people. If a dog doesn't like a guy, it's a certain sign that a woman should beware. Quite a few responders maintained that their dogs had always been right in showing displeasure: these men later turned out to be bad news when it came to relationships.

Janet Graham, a photographer from South Bend, Indiana, managed to pursue two relationships via the Internet. Online announcements about animals in trouble inspired her to volunteer to help transport dogs from shelters to approved homes where they would be fostered or adopted. This endeavor ultimately led to having a new dog in her life. She also began a six-year long-distance relationship with Pete, a man she met online.

The Indy Great Pyrenees Rescue organization asked Janet to transport Lady, a female Great Pyrenees, from Kentucky to Indianapolis. Janet was eager to rescue Lady from a shelter where the dog would have been euthanized. Pete accompanied her to pick up this sweet, shy dog at a gas station, and he immediately warned Janet not to get too attached to Lady. In his unasked-for opinion, Janet didn't need a dog. Several months later, after Lady's new home didn't work out, the dog made her way back to Janet to become a family pet. Pete never did have much use for Lady. But the dog's loving nature inspired Janet's rescuing spirit, and soon she plunged wholeheartedly into the world of fostering homeless pets.

Although Janet's relationship with her boyfriend continued, Lady, who usually adored people, made it clear that she didn't like Pete. Janet says, "When Pete was around, Lady charged at him like a ram. She never did this to anyone else." Janet's friends began questioning whether Lady was trying to warn her about Pete and cautioned Janet that dogs are great judges of character. Eventually, Janet listened to her dog and considered all the other problems she was having with Pete, such as difficulties with his teenager. The two split up — a decision Janet never regretted.

Now Janet says, "Within the first few days of meeting him, I always let Lady evaluate the man I'm thinking of dating. If she disapproves, I have learned that there is a reason and I need to move on. Once Lady did a body block on me while I tried to give a man a hug, and she would not allow him to pet her. I had already decided he wasn't right for me. I love that girl!"

Some women, however, believe that a dog responds to projections of the woman's unconscious. They theorize that an angry dog, for example, picks up on the unexpressed feelings of an angry woman and acts them out. Certainly Sigmund Freud would have agreed with that point of view. He used to have dogs assist him in discerning what his patients were really thinking.[9]

With the aid of the Internet, women meet dog-loving men through matchmaking sites that predict compatible relationships between males and females. Datemypet.com, Mustlovepets.com, Doglover.biz, Therightbreed.com, Petpeoplemeet.com, and Love melovemypets.com are some of the websites that help dog enthusiasts find each other.

Dogs don't need Internet dating sites, though, to create sympatico human couples. Jessica Murray of Nashville, Tennessee, met a new boyfriend while taking Scooby, her three-year-old, seventy-five-pound Doberman, to Wrigley Field in the heart of Chicago. One day, Jessica noticed the most beautiful Doberman she'd ever seen, one with black and rust coloring and perfectly cut ears. She walked around the dog park, trying to find out who belonged to this dog.

She noticed a man wearing a Red Sox T-shirt and cap. Jessica used to live in Boston and was a big fan of the team. Since she wore a similar Red Sox T-shirt that day, she walked over to the man at the same time that the Doberman she admired also approached him. She and the man struck up a conversation. Turns out his dog, Micah, was a trained search-and-rescue K-9.

The two Doberman lovers' encounter at the dog park extended into an evening date. A few months later, when the man moved to Nashville, Jessica went with him. Jessica says, "We had a big, happy family with two Dobermans, one Belgian Malinois, and one Chihuahua." Although the romance didn't last, Jessica and this man continued their friendship. All of this was made possible by finding mutuality at a Chicago dog park.

Sometimes dogs bring people together even when it's the result of a dog's odd behavior. Such was the case with Flavia Bellu of Berkeley, California. Her neighbor's tan and white Australian shepherd–Australian cattle dog, Zippy, always barked sharply at Flavia whenever she returned home. The dog belonged to Nancy, an older woman with a bad back and knee pain who often couldn't walk Zippy.

Nancy had rented the cottage behind her house to a handsome man named Jake. One day, Flavia was out in her yard and started chatting with Jake over the fence. She mentioned that she wished Zippy would be more relaxed around her. Jake suggested that the three of them take a walk together.

Flavia says, "Zippy won my heart on that first walk. Subsequently, Zippy and I took more than a thousand walks together. I loved seeing him rolling in the grass in the sun and romping around with other dogs, jubilant and free. These were some of the most joyful moments of my life." Flavia's walks with Zippy also resulted in a friendship with Jake that bloomed into an eight-year romance. She says, "We like to think Zippy introduced us." Although the romance didn't lead to marriage, Flavia and Jake remain good friends.

In general, the women who answered the question about the ways dogs and men influence their relationships agreed that a dog could offer important clues about a man's character. If a man didn't like a woman's dog, she would be more inclined to part with the man than to ditch the dog. On a more positive note, several respondents told stories about men who hadn't liked dogs or hadn't wanted a dog at first, but who grew to be best buddies with the new family member.

And then there are the men who totally get a woman's love and devotion to dogs. The result can be a romance with a happy ending.

Karen Minton of Elizabethtown, Kentucky, was divorced when she met Phil in spring 2009. The fact that Karen had five rescued dogs tended to scare off other men, but not Phil.

Whenever he visited her house, Phil made a point of greeting the dogs first by petting each one and sitting on the floor to play with them.

In September 2009, an animal rescuer asked Karen if she could adopt another pug, named Lucy, and Phil offered to help care for the dog. Now when Karen visits Phil's house, she brings several of her

Karen and Phil with Karen's six rescued dogs

dogs, and he stocks toys, water bowls, and snacks for them. The pugs shed a lot, but Phil keeps lint brushes in his truck and house and doesn't complain about dog hair on his furniture. He accompanies Karen to the veterinarian when one of the dogs is sick.

Karen says, "I am not quite sure where this relationship is going, but Phil has been fully accepted into my little fur family, and it's a good thing. I made it clear from the beginning that we are a package deal, and he didn't run away."

Welcome to Dog-Plus-Woman World

Americans have 73 million dogs in their homes, and most consider their dogs to be family members. You are about to meet more than twenty amazing dogs who have become friends, playmates, teachers, and healers, and the generous women who were privileged to have these trustworthy and honest beings grace their lives. We invite you to read more about the contributing authors at the back of this book. They have graciously shared aspects of their cherished bonds with dogs.

You may recognize your own dealings with canine companions in these pages as the stories touch on the themes of dogs' unwavering loyalty and their ability to heal and inspire us in amazing ways. We have included a meditation after each story as a prompt to aid you in reflecting, if you wish, on the themes in the contributing author's experiences that parallel those in your life.

The following women, like all the other women in this book, have reaped emotional, physical, and spiritual benefits from caring for dogs and receiving unconditional love in return.

- Rosanne Nordstrom tells a Chicago-based story reminiscent of the popular movie *The Blind Side*. Her journey began when her Newfoundland-Labrador mix, a rescued dog, brought her together with an impoverished yet resourceful child who would become like a son to her.
- Lori Stevens offers the inspiring story of a rescued black Lab named Beau, who has been featured on *NBC Nightly News*, *Late Night with David Letterman*, and the Animal Planet network. Beau helped Lori start the nonprofit organization Patriot PAWS, which carefully matches specially trained dogs with disabled veterans, and he also helped her raise funds for it.

- Karen Dawn, author of *Thanking the Monkey* (Harper-Collins, 2008) and founder of the animal advocate organization DawnWatch, expresses the beauty and sorrow of saying good-bye to her beloved dog of twelve years, Buster Dawn. She conveys thoughts and feelings that women who love dogs sometimes experience when others denigrate the value of a relationship that remains unmatched in its purity and honesty.

- Marilyn Walton writes the uplifting story of Janet Ballard, national award–winning police dog trainer, and her rescued dog, Major, who found his first love and a home with Janet. In return Major saved Janet's life while serving as her K-9 partner. This artfully crafted story, with its positive messages, was the grand prize (first place) winner of the 2009 Dogs and the Women Who Love Them True Story Contest sponsored by Angel Animals Network.

- Kim Dudek introduces her rescued pit bull Dagnabit, who had previously been tortured as part of his training for dogfights in New Orleans. He inspired Kim to found Dag's House, where she and her staff specialize in the shelter, fitness, and rehabilitation of special needs dogs.

- Barbara Techel shares the story of her journey with Frankie, a dog who won't let using a doggie wheelchair stop her from visiting schools and vigorously living life to the fullest. Frankie demonstrates that having disabilities or being different doesn't necessarily put limitations on fulfilling your mission and following your dreams.

Join us as we enter a world where dogs and women treat each other with the utmost respect and gratitude. It is our honor to introduce incredible dogs who have ignited the passions of extraordinary women and enabled them to embrace life and find joy in the moment.

ONE

Loyalty

We have our spot.
Each night she waits for my
"Say-up," flying weightless
Into a clump of soft hair
Warming my feet up on the couch.
Slipping into the comfort of
Old marrieds, content with
Nearness and routine.
I reach down and squeeze her foot
In our secret shake. She eyes me,
flops over, sighs.
God is nigh.

— JANICE A. FARRINGER, "Comfort Zone"

More Than a Guide Dog

Sally Rosenthal, PHILADELPHIA, PENNSYLVANIA

As a guide dog handler, I have found that most people know what these working dogs provide for those of us who are blind. We rely on the special training and highly developed intelligence of our canine partners to help us travel safely and independently, and we appreciate the way guide dogs serve as icebreakers in social situations.

Boise, my first guide dog from Guiding Eyes for the Blind, retired unexpectedly due to liver disease and went to live with her beloved puppy raisers, Judy and Skip, just a few hours away. For several months after Boise retired, I was without a guide dog. I had often joked that Boise, a very smart black Labrador with a decidedly independent and humorous nature, would be a hard act for any dog to follow. Yet I wasn't apprehensive about welcoming a new guide dog into my life and heart. I knew that the staff at Guiding Eyes were selecting a dog from the school's kennel of top-notch Labradors to match my lifestyle and physical needs, and training the dog to work specifically with me. I realized that, because of these things, I would easily make the transition from Boise to her successor.

I missed the independence a guide dog gave me. I looked forward to, before long, having a harness handle in my hand again and a trusted canine companion to guide me confidently. Together we would shop for groceries, take part in church activities, and do our part to keep a local coffee shop in business with frequent stops for coffee for me and a few ice cubes for the dog who lay quietly under the table.

When I was matched with Greta, I knew that having another dog by my side would assure me all the safety, mobility, and social interaction I had enjoyed with Boise. What I didn't know when this new, almost three-year-old petite yellow Labrador retriever entered my life was that Greta was more than just an ordinary guide dog. She was, as I came to learn, a dog with many missions.

I was not the first woman Greta had loved and helped. Like all potential guide dogs born in the kennel maintained by Guiding Eyes for the Blind, Greta spent the first year or so of her life with a puppy raiser. This is an individual who teaches the dog basic obedience commands, perfects house manners, and begins the socialization process. Most puppies go to a network of puppy-raiser volunteers for training, but Greta was among a small number who were loaned to Puppies Behind Bars (PBB), an organization that places puppies for various assistance dog programs with prison inmates.

Based in New York City, Puppies Behind Bars works with a number of prisons whose male or female inmates are specifically selected to take part in this program. I don't know how Greta was chosen to become a PBB pup, so I can only imagine. As a gregarious puppy with a willingness to please, she no doubt responded to the love and commitment the program ensured for all its puppies and inmates. Having passed a rigorous screening process, inmates in this program participate in structured training with their puppies on weekdays. Community volunteers provide the puppies with additional training and exposure to the world outside prison walls on weekends.

Although I have had no direct contact with Greta's puppy

raiser, I do know that these inmates value their work with the puppies for a number of reasons. For many, the loving bond they form with the puppies is the first unconditional love they have experienced. Raising a potential assistance dog builds their self-esteem, often causing them to feel as though they have made a positive contribution to society. When Greta left the PBB program to return to Guiding Eyes for the Blind and embark on her formal guide dog training, she no doubt left behind a woman who was changed for the better.

All of Guiding Eyes' working guide dogs are among the best in the field because of an excellent breeding program and dedicated trainers. I believe Greta benefited from her involvement in the PBB program. Her exposure to many new experiences and people — her prison experiences and weekend activities with a variety of volunteers — no doubt helped shape her personality and abilities.

After completing her formal guide dog training at Guiding Eyes, Greta arrived at my home with her Guiding Eyes trainer for ten days of intensive training with me. From the moment I opened my front door and bent down to touch Greta's head and give her a kiss, which she exuberantly returned in Labrador fashion, I felt a special bond with her. It strengthened as we trained. Our instructor commented on how quickly we became attached to each other and began our partnership.

Greta's Mission Expands

Greta's puppy raiser and I were not the only women whose lives were changed by the intervention of this sweet and loving dog. Shortly after Greta and I became a guide dog team in 2007, my elderly mother entered hospice care in a nursing home. Because my father had died peacefully under hospice care several years earlier, I knew my mother would also experience the end of life with the same dignity. On our first visit to the nursing home together, I told Greta we were going to visit her grandmother.

Upon entering the room my mother shared with three other patients, Greta immediately guided me to her even though they had never met. My mother was sitting in a chair when we arrived. Greta placed her front paws on my mother and kissed her as if the two of them had been lifelong friends. Although this sort of greeting wasn't one I would have encouraged in a working guide dog, in this instance I felt entirely comfortable with Greta's gently enthusiastic greeting. It marked the beginning of a special connection she and my mother, a true dog lover, would share.

Sally's Greta

As my mother's fragile health declined, visits from Greta were among her few remaining joys. The dog always seemed to know if my mother needed a gentle Labrador head on her lap or a visit filled with more interaction, such as when my mother gave Greta tummy rubs.

Because mothers worry about their children until their dying day, my own mother remained concerned about me and how I would cope with blindness in middle age. She often worried about my physical safety as I walked and traveled and, like me, was concerned about how blindness made many daily tasks more difficult and time-consuming. I knew she was letting go of worry and life when, at the end of one visit, she leaned over and told Greta, "You take good care of my Sally." Seeing how well Greta and I worked together enabled my mother to die more peacefully.

My mother's assessment of Greta's skills was absolutely correct. While all guide dog teams undergo strenuous training together, Greta had been given even more specialized training to work with me. Due to a stroke in infancy, I have some physical disabilities in addition to the blindness I have experienced for the past decade. Greta was one of a selective group of guide dogs at Guiding Eyes for the Blind who had advanced training in that organization's special needs program. This meant she was able to work with a visually impaired handler who also has other disabilities.

During our first two years together, Greta learned to guide on my right side to compensate for my left-sided weakness, walk at a slower pace than most guide dogs, and help keep me walking in a straight line. She did all these things in addition to the usual and often stressful guide work, proving what an excellent dog she is. With Greta's guidance, I was able to continue my daily routine of errands, leisure activities, and church involvement.

As I had done with Boise, I was able to walk confidently and with more physical ease because of Greta's understanding of both my visual and special mobility needs. Greta, with her guide dog training and her sensitivity, quickly assessed our teamwork and made any needed adjustments in her guiding. I told her often that she was the world's best guide dog, and I feel certain she agreed.

Therapy Dog Greta

Seeing how well Greta interacted with my mother in the nursing home made me think that she would be, as Boise had been, a good pet therapy dog. Soon after my mother died, Greta and I became pet therapy volunteers in two local nursing homes with Pals For

Life, a pet therapy organization located in suburban Philadelphia. Just as she had with my mother, Greta charmed ill and lonely residents. She was always ready to greet depressed elderly residents with a wagging tail and a head just waiting to be patted. Her Labrador cheerfulness brightened everyone's day.

As we celebrated the second anniversary of our partnership, I thought there would be few challenges left for Greta to undertake. However, life proved me wrong. I was diagnosed with lymphedema resulting from lifelong physical problems associated with many orthopedic surgeries. I spent a number of months going for outpatient treatment at a nearby rehabilitation hospital. During my treatments Greta slept peacefully, and when we had lunch in the hospital cafeteria, she garnered legions of admirers. I have been told that Greta is an especially pretty dog, with her dark yellow coat and brown ears and tail. People at the hospital were quick to comment on her beauty and excellent guide work in a crowded cafeteria. Greta, lying calmly under the table as I ate my lunch, was a model guide dog in repose.

Because lymphedema is a permanent condition that, in my case, has caused some gait changes, Greta has continued to adapt her guide skills to my needs. She refines them as necessary in order to keep us involved in all our customary activities. Lymphedema wrappings can be bulky. Sensing my difficulty with the wrappings, and recognizing that tiredness sometimes slows down my walking, Greta adjusts her pace as she guides me. She is, according to my husband, taking extra care while guiding me around obstacles such as grates and speed bumps on our early-morning walks at our condominium complex. I am impressed that she is so attuned to my needs.

Greta and I will soon train as hospice volunteers. While visiting my father in an in-patient hospice several years ago, I learned that the facility welcomed weekly visits from a therapy dog. I thought about how much I would like to someday offer the solace of a dog of my own, not knowing at the time that the dog in question would be a guide dog. Given her penchant for seeking out those in need, Greta, I am certain, will be on yet another mission.

MEDITATION

Dogs, like people, can have several missions in life. What multiple talents in dogs and yourself could you make use of and expand on to find more joy and purpose?

K-9 Major — from Chains to Heroism

Marilyn Walton, NEW ALBANY, OHIO

One bitter Wisconsin day in a blinding snowstorm, a young German shepherd was born in a snowbank. The only puppy to survive his litter, he nuzzled against his mother for warmth and protection from the cruel wind.

As he grew old enough to leave his mother, a rural Wisconsin family adopted him for the sole purpose of protecting their farm. They named the young dog Major. Clearly, they wanted a demonstrative warrior and chose the name accordingly. Major's job was to scare strangers off the property, so the family fostered aggression in the dog by giving him very little human contact. The training worked only too well, and the family eventually came to fear the dog. When he became more aggressive than they had anticipated, family members didn't know how to deal with the threatening creature they had created.

Major was chained to a stake on the run-down premises, where no family member cared about him or dared to stop by to break the monotony of his long days. The family did not want the dog running away, so he remained tethered. Loss of a property protector was their only concern, not loss of a cherished animal. Constantly chained and never properly socialized, Major became even more aggressive as the weeks and months passed by.

While biting winter wind howled across the plain, lonely Major survived each day without the warmth or protection of a doghouse. A snowy lump of fur, he hunkered down against the cold. For two years, Major had no one to play with and trusted no one. He suffered through the hard winters with ragged, frostbitten ears. Children with sticks teased the thin and sickly dog, even when he tried to eat his meager dinner. He always remembered their cruelty and would never feel close to children.

Janet Ballard (née Koch) had recently been honorably discharged from the army. Despite the fact that she was awarded an Army Commendation Medal upon her discharge, she left the military with some sadness. She had been forced to leave behind her bomb detection–patrol dog, Duke, a German shepherd she had grown to love so much and still missed. Duke had been trained by the Military Working Dog Foundation. For three and a half years, Janet had handled MWD Duke in Washington, D.C. During her time of service with Duke, she had been promoted to kennel master and sergeant in charge of her unit. Her slight frame and easy smile belied her expertise in training and handling the toughest dogs. She was young but self-assured, and her sense of humor was an asset that eased her way among fellow soldiers, just as her gentle but firm approach won over the dogs in her charge.

After returning to civilian life, Janet wanted to continue working with dogs. She took a job with the Jackson County Sheriff's Department in Wisconsin and convinced the sheriff to let her train a dog on her own time to perform K-9 duties. He gave his permission to bring any good dog she found to him for inspection and approval.

Janet's friend Ruth knew the woman who had adopted Major's father — a beautiful German shepherd dog named Caesar, who was living a happy life with loving people. The woman had told Ruth the story of lonely Major and expressed hope that someone would be able to help the dog. When Janet heard about Major from Ruth, she arranged to meet the dog. "I was looking for a dog who had the potential to be as good as Duke, but I knew that those would be big paws to fill. My new dog would need heart and courage, and he would have to love to play fetch."

The woman who had Caesar brought Major to Ruth's farm so that Janet could test the dog on neutral territory. From a distance, Janet saw that Major had the potential to be a beautiful dog like Caesar, but that he looked very sad and appeared to be in bad shape — he was underfed and in poor health. There was no glow to his heavy, matted coat.

Ruth and the woman took the scruffy dog into the barn and fastened his chain to a stake. Purposely dressed in unusual clothing — a floppy hat and long, oversized coat — Janet suddenly appeared before the startled dog. Her goal was to create a bit of agitation and determine his level of defense and "prey drive," the basic drive for survival in dogs derived from their past in the wild, where they had to chase after their dinners. Janet watched for the modern-day equivalent of a prey drive by observing how interested the dog was in chasing a ball, toy, person, or whatever else she meant for the dog to catch.

A lot was riding on the initial testing result, because Janet would take Major home with her if he tested well. To Janet's delight, Major responded boldly by barking and snarling with extreme confidence, matching her aggressive behavior with his own.

Once Major had passed his first test, Janet took him outside the barn for further testing. She moved slowly around the dog to observe him. After a cursory assessment, she moved farther away and peeked at him from behind some trees to test his reactions. The dog growled and barked ferociously.

"Perfect!" Janet thought. "Now let's see what he's got." Slowly, Janet removed her odd clothing while talking softly to Major. She took her time, letting the dog get more comfortable with her as she watched his aggression start to dissipate. Despite his former unfriendly response, Janet slowly inched closer. Suddenly, his fierceness ceased completely. As Janet drew near enough to stroke him with her gentle hand, Major's heart melted. She squatted down to address him at his level, and he put his massive, furry head into Janet's lap. He allowed her to scratch him, enjoying a tactile luxury he'd surely never known on the farm.

Janet felt an instant bond with the dog. Memories of her beloved Duke momentarily flooded back as she looked at the scraggly dog with his head still burrowing into her lap. He needed her so badly. Without a moment's hesitation, she decided to keep him. "As soon as I took his leash, he easily went with me, watching me all the time, alert at my side."

Finally freed from his dreaded chain and stake, Major trotted along, eager to enter Janet's car. He was so excited to go with her that he jumped right in. Once inside the car, he barked at anyone who tried to get near Janet. "Already, he felt the need to protect me, but he responded with trust when I told him everything was okay."

Major Meets the Sheriff

Janet drove Major directly to the sheriff to show him her new dog. Boldly, the dog strutted into the building. "Even though Major obviously had had a rough start in life, he exhibited the same self-confidence I had seen in his father, Caesar. Nothing seemed to scare him."

Finding no one in the sheriff's office, fun-loving Janet sat behind her boss's desk with the dog at her side. When the sheriff returned, the startled Major leapt up from the floor and jumped over the desk. Janet caught him on the other side before the big dog could chase the sheriff down the hall. The shocked look on the man's face was funny to Janet; she laughed at Major attempting to run the sheriff out of his own office. Major had surprised her as well, since she had never expected him to go over the desk.

The sheriff too laughed heartily. Being a dog lover, he knew that he and Major would become fast friends. He instantly admired Major's spirit and sensed the same potential that Janet had seen in the dog.

Afterward, as Janet drove Major to his new home, she considered the value the dog could add to her department. Her previous experience running the 561st Military Police company in Ft. Myer, Virginia, under the Military District of Washington had taught her what to look for in a good dog, and Major fit that mold. "Major seemed to have all the qualities I was looking for. He was fearless, protective, responsive, and confident and had a superb prey drive. I knew Major had to be a fighter to have survived his early life and emerge with the ability to trust people and learn new skills. And who could resist those adoring brown eyes?"

As Janet pulled into her driveway, Major curiously observed all that he saw in the yard. With much interest he explored the house before receiving his first dinner. Janet suspected that the dog had worms and nutritional problems, so at dinnertime she tenderly fed him a bowl of warm, cooked rice mixed with cottage cheese. She wanted to give him something that would be easy on his stomach. Major savored each bite, enjoying his meal in peaceful surroundings far from his austere farmyard. For the first time, someone cared for him. That night, he bounded onto Janet's waterbed and curled up next to her, touching his thick, bristly, black and gold outdoor coat to her back. "It didn't take long for Major to enjoy the benefits of being an indoor dog. He loved to lie with his back pressed against mine. Our trust in each other built quickly."

A Working Partnership

The working partnership between Janet and Major had begun, and it would be a long journey for the dog who had been so deprived. He made progress in incremental steps. His first days included a series of severe stomach upsets, and such episodes would continue to plague him for most of his life. His coat remained dull, lacking the sheen of a healthy shepherd, and his ears needed constant care to attempt to correct the damage that subzero temperatures had inflicted on the unprotected and vulnerable animal. For months, Janet fed him a gentle diet and kept his ears warm. Ever so slowly, his thick fur coat began to shine.

"I began training him very quickly to get his mind occupied and to continue building our bond. There were many things he had to learn, but obedience was first." Janet used the ball that was one of Major's favorite toys to play fetch, which encouraged him to respond properly to her. "He loved the game and really started to come out of his shell." Major was particularly fond of a metal chain that held Janet's squad car keys. Chasing after it when Janet threw the key chain was great fun for a dog who had seldom played. He welcomed anything that belonged to Janet.

In order to build up his strength, Janet constructed an agility course in her backyard and started teaching Major to jump, crawl, and climb. "Agility training was one of his favorite things to do — he loved the freedom of racing the course."

Major matured, and after gradual training he was able to scale straight up an eleven-foot wall. Loving care was what he needed in order to cure most of what had ailed him physically and emotionally. A happy spirit replaced the saddened display that Janet had seen at the farm. As his sensitive stomach began to settle and he could absorb Janet's nutritious meals, the hairless tips of Major's ears also healed and filled in. He was finally taking on the appearance of a true German shepherd. "I knew his stomach was getting better when he ran to his bowl, picked it up, brought it to me, and dropped it in my lap. That was a hint I couldn't miss."

For all the hardships the dog had endured in the first two years of life, he still had heart and courage. He was so grateful to Janet for saving him and offering him a happy home that he would do anything for her. Whenever anyone, friend or relative, came near Janet or tried to touch her, Major ran to her side and offered his protection. He strove to do his job to the best of his ability, and protecting Janet was the number one task as far as he was concerned. It was a habit the dog never broke. "Major made it clear what the rules were for people who came close to us. He was fine with hugs from people he knew, but he did not like anyone grabbing me or roughhousing. He never bit anyone he wasn't supposed to, but he made it clear what the boundaries were. My husband always joked that before he married me, it was amazing that I'd had any dates with protective Major around."

Serious Training

At two years of age, Major was sufficiently old enough to begin serious training for police work. Because he was a natural at figuring out concepts, his training progressed quickly.

Major *loved* to work and he *lived* to work. Soon, he was chasing and holding decoy "bad guys" in training and learning to respond unquestioningly to Janet's loud commands. "I initially used positive motivators, such as a ball or other toy, to speed his training. When we started criminal apprehension work, he put his heart and soul into it but always released the decoy immediately when I told him to let go. When trained to do a recall — where the dog is sent out to apprehend someone but is called back before he actually does so — he was always obedient and would turn on a dime. I never saw a dog who 'got it' the way Major did."

Major was incredibly alert — always observant and missing nothing. When they trained, the curious dog watched as Janet slipped a heavily padded sleeve onto a decoy who was supposed to be apprehended. The sleeve, made of burlap and padding, was laced along the inside of the arm of an officer posing as a "bad guy," and it protected the wearer from the dog's mouth pressure and tooth punctures. When Janet first told Major to grab the sleeve, he responded as if he had done this all his life. When she taught him new commands, he did everything right on the first try. He was the easiest dog she had ever trained, after previously training eighteen of them in her military kennel.

As soon as Major had some basic obedience training, he went with Janet in the patrol car so she could train with him at other locations and expose him to the types of smells, sights, and sounds he would encounter when he worked. "Major's place was in the back of the squad car, behind a barrier. A sliding gate let him stick his head into the front of the car to get petted and watch what was going on." In that position, his observation skills intensified.

Whenever Janet entered the car, Major stared at the ignition quizzically, waiting for her to insert the key that dangled from her silver key chain. Then he would look at the brake pedal as if anticipating that she would step on it. As she did, his eyes moved to the gearshift and then to the steering wheel. "I just noticed one day that Major would whine when I put my foot on the brake. I watched him when I went through the sequence of starting the car. He knew all the steps in order. He proved to me again how smart he was and that he had reasoning ability."

After Major graduated from training, the two became official police partners. Being in the car and patrolling with Janet brought true contentment to the dog. At the end of each shift, Janet filed a report on their nightly activities. "Major absolutely loved the car and riding in it. I wish he could have learned to write reports. They probably would have been better than mine!"

Major developed a fondness for chasing and catching skunks, much to Janet's dismay. Whether camping with Janet or on official police business and conducting a search, he encountered many of the black and white curiosities. No matter how many times he was "skunked," he still pursued them. In his old farm surroundings, restricted by his tether, he had always found skunks to be just beyond his reach. Now the playing field had been leveled, and skunks were fair game. Casting risk aside, he was determined to chase them. But in reality, the humans he chased were far more dangerous.

The Perils of Policing

While working the night shift, Janet and Major patrolled Wisconsin's most forbidding streets — ones that were always fraught with danger. Late one evening, they stopped at a location where two drunken loggers fought in the street. "Break it up and go home!" Janet ordered from her car.

As she tried to drive away, one of the men clung to her car window and was dragged along by the moving vehicle. Janet slammed on the brakes and radioed for help. Leaving Major in the car, she stepped out to arrest the drunken men. Then a struggle broke out. In his small K-9 compartment behind the driver's seat, Major nervously paced back and forth and barked as he watched helplessly. He knew the steps for starting the car but not how to extricate himself from it.

Janet had clicked one handcuff on the first belligerent man's wrist when the second man sneaked up behind her and grabbed for her gun. She whirled around to stop him. The first man slashed wildly with her dangling handcuffs. She sprayed both men with mace and ran to release Major. The second man stood out of the way and waited cooperatively.

"I'm not afraid of that dog!" the first drunken man roared.

But he should have been. With tremendous speed and ferocity, Major exited the car, leapt up, and knocked the man down. The dog held the man on the ground until other officers arrived to make arrests. "You never would have got me without that dog!" the first man yelled as he was being dragged away.

The next day Janet saw one of the men at the police station, now sober and calm. "That's some dog you've got," he said happily. "Can I pet him?"

Major let out a low, persistent, and threatening growl. He chose not to be petted by someone who had tried to harm Janet. "I was so very proud of Major and thankful that he had been on the scene. I knew I was in big trouble and would not have escaped the incident unscathed. I had lost control of the situation and could have been quickly overpowered."

All the training and trust had paid off. Major proved his worth many times over and reinforced Janet's belief that she was wise to have taken a chance on him. "A lot of people will respect the dog just because of his mere presence, but not these guys. The dog was simply a challenge to them. Major had to prove that his bite was worse than his bark and change their minds about continuing the fight." And that, he clearly did.

Mortal Danger

After many routine nights on patrol, Janet got a call directing her to locate a very troubled man who had escaped from a mental hospital elsewhere in Wisconsin. It was the middle of the night, and he had driven around aimlessly for four hours, eventually entering Jackson County. He had been taking powerful prescription medicine and illegal drugs that combined to make him agitated and very strong.

In the misty night, Janet could hear gravel crunch beneath her tires as she drove slowly at the edge of a busy highway and eased to a stop. She rolled her window down for a better view. The sound of Major's panting broke the occasional moments of silence when traffic subsided, and they waited in the quiet car to watch and listen for the troubled man.

Janet spotted a car parked on the side of the freeway, straddling the shoulder line. With her squad car's lights flashing, she got out, approached the suspicious car, and investigated it cautiously. The suspect bolted from his car and ranted in unintelligible gibberish. Janet could not communicate with him at all. Unexpectedly he turned and ran out into traffic just as a semi-trailer barreled straight toward him.

With Major still in the car, Janet raced after the man. She grabbed him by the back of his shirt and pulled him back so the truck would not hit him. Major was frantic at being locked in the car. He barked and paced in nervous frustration. The man spun around. He swung wildly, striking Janet behind her left ear. The blow sent her crashing to the ground, and she briefly lost consciousness. As she came to, she saw the man running.

"Stop!" Janet screamed and scrambled to her feet. But the man paid no attention to her and continued to run. "Stop, or I'll send the dog!"

Instead of stopping, the man doubled back toward Janet as she reached for her squad car door to let Major out. Once again, Janet warned the man to stop, but to no avail. With no further options available to her, Janet flung open the door and sent Major to apprehend him. The eager dog took off in a flash.

Major's large padded feet drummed down the freeway shoulder at top speed. Then he leapt upward, flew through the air as he was trained to do, and lunged for the man's left arm. With his right hand, the suspect reached under Major's chin and grabbed the attacking dog's choke-chain collar, stopping Major's forward progress. The dog struggled valiantly, utilizing all his strength in an attempt to apprehend the man. With drug-induced power, the man twisted the choke chain. The dog had never encountered such a life-threatening situation. The vision seemed to play out before Janet's eyes in a surreal, slow progression of increasingly horrifying moments.

The man yanked the dog from midair down to the ground, where they continued to struggle. Janet ran to catch up to them. When she got there, Major was attempting, unsuccessfully, to grab the man but was losing ground quickly. With all her strength, Janet struck at the hand twisting Major's chain to get the man to release the dog. As she reached to strike the crazed man's arm, Major lunged at him once again. Janet's arm and Major's mouth intersected, and she received a bite to her forearm that crippled her momentarily. "Major!" Janet yelled, and he immediately released her arm.

The brief interruption of his momentum caused the poor dog to struggle even harder, but he was losing the fight. All three fell to the ground. Defeated, Major finally passed out.

Janet knew she would be the agitated man's next target. Sick with worry about her partner, she put a "sleeper hold" on the man. With this nonlethal submission hold designed to gain compliance, Janet exerted pressure on the man's carotid arteries, which decreased the blood flow to his brain and rendered him temporarily unconscious. She kept constant pressure on his neck. He slowly released his grip on the unconscious dog, who lay unmoving on the cold ground. Afraid to let go lest the man wake up and restart the fight, Janet maintained her hold on him until help arrived moments later.

After the other officers took the suspect away, Janet's first order of business was to make sure her partner was okay. She watched with some trepidation as Major slowly regained consciousness.

Once he was breathing normally, he jumped up and his eyes darted back and forth, looking for more action. Janet checked him over carefully, and he seemed to be fine. With great relief, she hugged him close. "Thank you, thank you," she said to her loyal dog as she clung to him. Words were not adequate to convey what was in her heart.

The officers took Janet to the hospital so she could be treated for her dog bite and the knot behind her ear from the blow to her head. She knew that the bite was her fault and not Major's, and she hoped he knew it too. But more important, the dog had saved her from what could have become a fight to the death. Her wounds were treated, and miraculously Major required no veterinary care. The dog had not been violently taken from her by the crazed man, and that was all that really mattered.

The thought of losing Major was unbearable to Janet. The refrain "what if" kept running through her mind as she contemplated how close they had both come to dying. Without Major, she would have been the man's main target. With his drug-induced strength, the confrontation would have likely ended with deadly consequences.

After analyzing the entire incident, Janet knew she never wanted to have anything like it repeated. She purchased a special collar for Major, and from that day on he trotted proudly by her side sporting a black leather collar with sharp silver spikes to prevent anyone from grabbing his vulnerable neck. It served him well during his years working in Wisconsin, and he wore it just as proudly when the team eventually moved to Minnesota.

Out of Commission

When routine veterinary care was sometimes required for Major, he had his qualms about it. Even though over time Major was much friendlier and trusting with Janet's friends and family, he was still wary of doctors. Janet always made sure she was present for all veterinary procedures. "Major just wasn't fond of people 'messing' with him."

His need for her was sorely tested once when Major was struck with mysterious medical symptoms. He had grown to be a healthy dog, but one day before work he refused to eat. Normally he had a good appetite and left no crumbs in his bowl, so this time Janet knew something was amiss. On their way to work, once he had been in the car for a few minutes, he vomited, and Janet became concerned. When Major grew more and more lethargic, she took him to the local veterinarian, who thought he simply had an upset stomach. The doctor gave Janet some medication for him and sent the pair away.

By the next night, Major was much sicker, and Janet took him to an emergency veterinary clinic. The dog was grumpy and snarly due to his pain by then, so the doctors did not want to touch him. At first, they suspected he might have an extremely serious condition called gastric torsion, or canine bloat, but after some discussion they determined he probably did not and sent him home.

The following night, Major's temperature was 108 degrees, and Janet could not get him to stand up — he just lay on the floor and cried. Janet loaded him into her squad car. Her nervous hands fumbled as she searched the silver key ring for the right key. With red lights flashing and sirens blaring, she drove him to the University of Minnesota Veterinary Medical Center. The doctors took him immediately and had him x-rayed. They confirmed that he had gastric torsion: his stomach had flipped over, trapping all its contents. The dog needed immediate, lifesaving surgery.

Although he was rapidly deteriorating, Major made it through surgery and was placed in intensive care. Tubes and catheters dangled from his limp body. The doctors kept him heavily sedated so he wouldn't disturb his incision and could tolerate the pain.

At first, Janet slept on the couch outside the ICU, but the vets were having difficulty getting Major to cooperate when they tried to care for him in his more lucid moments. The staff placed a sign on Major's cage that read: "DO NOT TOUCH THIS DOG!"

At this point, Janet moved into the veterinary ICU and stayed beside Major's cage. The vets showed her how to give the dog all the necessary care. Knowing her familiar hands and voice, Major

Janet Ballard and Major

never woke up when she tended to him. Only when the vets tried to administer treatment did he rouse himself and become surly.

A few days later, Janet took Major home, but he didn't seem to be recovering. He still refused to eat and to hold his favorite ball. In her heart, Janet knew that something was still wrong with her beloved dog. She gathered him up tenderly, placed him in her car, and returned him to the university veterinary clinic.

At the clinic, the doctors listened with compassion and examined the dog again. They decided to put a tube through his nose into his stomach to release the gas that was rapidly filling the empty cavity. But even though Major was sedated, each time they tried to thread the tube through his nose, he became highly agitated and began to growl. Janet asked if she could try, and the vets walked her through the procedure. Ever so carefully, she threaded the tube through Major's nose and down into his achy stomach. Major didn't make so much as a peep or open his eyes as long as it was Janet whose fingers were in front of his nose. He trusted her implicitly.

The procedure worked, and the dog finally got some relief from his pain. After Janet took him home, Major was like a new dog. He healed quickly. After a few weeks of trying to keep the energetic dog quiet, Janet took him back to work. "For years afterward, the vets at the university remembered Major's attitude and marveled at his ability to survive a bloat that went on so long without being treated." He had always shown her his heart, but once again he had shown his tremendous courage.

On the Trail of Bombs

Major continued to expand his career skills. Although he was trained as a patrol dog and to detect narcotics, when a position opened at a school in Minneapolis that trained dogs to detect explosives, Major and Janet enrolled. Major learned to distinguish the scent of a wide variety of often-complex explosive substances. He further learned to differentiate between the alert he should give when he found a bomb and the alert for finding drugs. In the past, he had been taught to scratch frantically at the location of detected drugs. Now he had to adopt a passive alert, which meant sitting quietly to indicate the presence of explosives without triggering an explosion. As always, he was an excellent student, and he graduated after completing all his classes.

With his new bomb-detection capability, Major was allowed to fly in the front cabins of airplanes with Janet. Whether traveling to national K-9 competitions and seminars or searching for narcotics or bombs in or around airplanes, Major increasingly found himself near planes and in them.

When he flew, Major curled up at Janet's feet and waited for flight attendants to bring him his own tray. The attendants were always delighted to see him and wanted to give him whatever Janet was having in addition to the treats she brought for him in her pocket. Major learned the excitement of takeoffs and logged many miles of domestic travel. Passengers often mistook him for a guide dog for the blind, since Janet dressed in plainclothes and Major traveled in the front cabin with no police I.D. Fellow travelers who watched them seemed puzzled when Janet pulled out a book to read without benefit of Braille.

Between flights, Major wandered through airports on a lead. Even when Janet went into the restroom, he felt he must watch out for her. Methodically slinking along the outside of the stalls, he'd thrust his furry head under the doors to greet many a startled woman. Knowing Major's curiosity, Janet always tried to find an empty restroom, which was seldom possible. More often, she had to take Major into a stall with her. Without fail, it seemed, someone would come in and take the stall right next to her. Major liked to say "hi," nosing under the divider and scaring the poor woman there half to death. "I think it was part of his sense of humor. Who would expect his enormous head poking under the stall divider at an airport?"

As Major continued his bomb- and drug-detection work, his career flourished. In time, he reached the pinnacle of success in the K-9 world: he was named Top Cop Dog in the nation in 1981 and came back to win again in 1982. Major's skill and accomplishments as a patrol dog enabled Janet Ballard (then named Janet Koch) to become the first female member to compete in the United States Police Canine Association Trials and the first person to win that prestigious competition two times in a row. She won two times with Major and then two more times at a later date with Major's replacement, K-9 Levi. No one had ever won four times, and to this day she is the only person to win the nationals four times with two different dogs. In addition, in the years she and her dogs did not take the number one spot, they consistently scored well enough in all the categories to remain winners in the top ten overall placements. Under Janet's tutelage, Major, Levi, and her final police dog, Wodon, continued her streak, winning more than a dozen regional dog trials in narcotics detection, bomb detection, and tracking.

A Fading Star

As Major aged, his body began to give out, even though his heart was still in the game. At last, Janet had to select a new German shepherd to become her partner. This time, she didn't want a dog with a temperament like Major's, because she knew she would always be comparing the two dogs. Major would be the gold standard, and the new dog would fall short of her expectations. She soon acquired her next dog, Levi, a German shepherd show dog known for his beauty. After training, Levi began to gradually fill in for Major and slowly took over his duties full-time.

For a while, Janet's old, loyal shepherd was good for a half-night's work, but she had to slowly wean him from coming to work at all. At age thirteen, he retired from service and stayed at Janet's home, anxiously awaiting her footsteps at the end of each shift.

Although the former police partners could no longer work together, they still played as any house pet and human companion would do. On cold snowy days, Janet's elderly furry friend eagerly used the regulation-size snow shovel she bought for him so he would stop trying to take hers. The old gentleman joyfully scooped up piles of snow and playfully flipped the cold white powder, the sort that long ago had stung his tender ears. It fell harmlessly on his back and covered Janet's freshly shoveled driveway. Snow was his enemy no more.

Janet still brought Major to training sessions and did gentle tasks with him — no more running through the agility course or demonstrating the flying bites he had been so proficient at during his earlier years. Major could continue his detection work to some degree, however. Investigators would often call and bring suspicious packages to Janet's house for Major to sniff, so the old fellow would not have to leave home. Janet had a regular workspace set up in her basement, where he worked on such tasks. He continued to do detection work almost until the end.

As the cold winds descended from Canada and dumped snow over Minnesota, Major rested snugly and warmly in retirement. He curled up and slept, dreaming whatever it is that old police dogs dream.

Major had served his partner and the department well. During his long career, he had once hit on $1.2 million in drug money, which eventually was divided among several police departments. In 1984, he became regional champion in the Top Cop Dog competition and placed fourth overall at nationals. At each regional competition to qualify for nationals, Major bested 60 dogs. At nationals, he competed against as many as 110 dogs.

Considering the accomplishments of the dog and his value to the police department, Major's replacement cost would have greatly exceeded twenty-five thousand dollars, the value calculated by adding up the officer hours necessary to train a dog to such a high level of expertise, the cost of the certifications he had earned, his vet bills, food, equipment, and other incidentals. But the objective price assigned to Major could not begin to compare with the subjective value Janet placed on her dog. To her, he was priceless.

Janet's skill in training K-9s continued to increase exponentially.

In 1983 and 1984, Levi, Major's replacement dog, took first place with Janet at the USPCA's National Field Trials. Janet became an expert witness in narcotics and patrol dog applications and established training and working relationships with the U.S. Secret Service, U.S. Customs, DEA, FBI, Minnesota Bureau of Criminal Apprehension, U.S. Postal Service, and numerous correctional facilities, airlines, and railroad authorities.

Janet Ballard is currently one of the most-respected police dog trainers in the country. Now that she has retired from police work, she concentrates on finding good dogs from animal shelters, and other rescued dogs, to train as narcotics and bomb detectors. She is expert at taking rescues from obscure pounds, humane societies, and dog rescue groups and transforming them into top-notch police service dogs. Three dog teams made up of dogs she has rescued, each dog paired with a highly trained officer, have gone on to become national champions in narcotics-detection competitions in recent years. Many times over, they have claimed regional championships, earning combined scores higher than those of any of the other teams that competed. In addition, Janet and her dogs have been among the top ten award winners for overall performance at the national USPCA trials.

Rescuing the dogs she selects for detector work has been the icing on the cake for Janet. She is gratified to see these dogs receive a second chance as she trains them at the Minneapolis–Saint Paul International Airport and surrounding metropolitan suburbs.

Major was, more than any other, the rescue she will never forget. A shabby, rural farm dog at the start, unchained Major started on the bottom and finished on top. It was love that drove him. He sped along in cars and flew across the country, but he always returned to what had been most elusive to him in his early life — a warm place called home.

Major taught Janet that the best dogs may not be the ones

with the highest pedigrees or most expensive and sophisticated training. The best dogs are driven by love and gratitude. They are thankful dogs who always return their human partner's appreciation willingly and without reserve. As her partner, Major was essential to Janet. His guidance was an integral part of her thinking process. He honed her training techniques, fulfilled her dreams, and warmed her heart. "We seemed to bond as one. Major always knew what I wanted, and I always knew what he needed. We did hundreds of demonstrations and call-outs. We jumped out of helicopters, crawled through swamps, searched for bombs, and protected each other from evil."

From the aggressive farmyard warrior who never had a toy, Major transformed into a noble gladiator who, when called to service, showed up ready to honor, protect, and defend. After he passed away in the warmth of his comfortable home, his ribbons, plaques, trophies, and an old, silver-colored squad car key ring remained to remind Janet of the valiant dog she was privileged to have had as her partner and friend. She would never find his equal.

MEDITATION

Teaming Janet and Major benefited them and countless people who were safer because of the partners' courage and bravery. What dog has been your loyal partner and spurred you to greatness?

A Working Girl Turned
Our Senior Center into a Family

Teresa Ambord, ANDERSON, CALIFORNIA

In my late thirties, I took a gamble and left the most disappointing job of my life — working as a county accountant — and accepted one of the lowest-paying but best jobs I would ever have as an adult. I knew there had to be more job satisfaction than what I was getting at the county. That's why, in 1994, I became the fiscal officer at a not-for-profit adult day-healthcare center for senior citizens in far northern California.

All the seniors who came to the center had physical problems that left them unable to take care of themselves. But most of them had hearts that had grown kinder as the years ticked by. I guess their own limitations had attuned them to the needs of others around them. If a staff member was out sick, the "participants," as we called them, were quick to notice and inquire about his or her well-being. Some would make get-well cards for us. One sweet man spent his days crafting beaded necklaces and bracelets for the female employees. I called them "high-fashion jewelry," and while we were at work most of us wore as many of his gifts as we could.

Sandy Goes to Work with Me

Several months into the job, I learned that some of the directors at the center were looking for a mascot. The only problem was that the dog would be alone on weekends at the center, and someone would have to come in and feed and walk the animal. As soon as I heard that, I knew I had a much better idea. My mild-mannered dog, Sandy, would be perfect since she was social enough to enjoy spending days among the seniors. So after getting the boss's approval, the very next day Sandy accompanied me to work.

The first morning, Sandy drew a lot of comments. Covered with long gray curls, she looked a bit unusual. It was almost as if she had been designed to blend perfectly with the gray heads that filled the center. She was a cross between an Australian shepherd and a terrier, and from behind she looked more like a small bear than a dog.

As we drove to the center each morning, Sandy didn't know she was a working girl. Going to work with me simply meant an early-morning ride followed by hours of miscellaneous activity as she made the rounds to be petted and cooed at by lonely people who loved her. These visits with the seniors were interrupted only by her intermittent long naps. And then at the end of the day, it was time for another ride in the car to go home.

I liked to say that Sandy went with me to earn her "bonies" (that was what I called the Milk-Bone dog biscuits I offered her). But to her, a day at the center resulted in one thing more important than all the snacks and attention. Going with me meant no waiting at home alone. No more listening for the sound of my car. No more sad eyes as I left in the morning. Now when I went to work, Sandy did too, and she stayed near me all day long — a perk for me that almost made up for the low salary that accompanied my not-for-profit job.

Ideal for the Job

I became pretty attached to the elderly people who spent their days at the center. This was something I had not expected, since my job did not involve direct contact with the participants. I handled the finances from a private office set apart from the recreation hall. But because of the building's layout, anytime I made a trip to the bathroom or to the kitchen for coffee, I passed through a roomful of seniors waiting for breakfast or lunch or preparing for some kind of activity.

Soon these people came to recognize my face, and as I walked through, they all wanted to say hello, hold my hand for a moment, and tell me some tidbit about their lives. Several times a week, they came to the center to socialize, eat hot meals, and get health checkups, physical therapy, and some form of recreation. But mostly they needed someone to listen to and care about them.

A few of the seniors seemed to be inching toward Alzheimer's. They didn't remember what had happened yesterday, but they might recall details from decades ago. They experienced a kind of mental fog that came and went. The time when these people could stay in their own houses had passed, so they had moved into group homes or were living with their children. Too often, this meant they'd had to leave behind well-loved cats or dogs, and this seemed to break their hearts more than any other loss. Some of the pets were adopted by the families of the elderly. Some were given to friends. Some had probably passed away years earlier, but the elderly people didn't realize the passage of time. One charming woman still spoke of the poodle she loved, as though the dog waited for her at home. I learned that the poodle had long since been given away, but she didn't know that, and none of us mentioned it.

Sandy was the ideal dog to ease the seniors' pain at losing their own pets, and she brightened the day of everyone who met her. She was eager to greet and be greeted in return, and she was not likely to jump on anyone. She even resembled the seniors in some ways. Like them, she moved slowly, seldom rushing to do anything.

Sandy and Food

Each morning Sandy would wait in the lobby for the first vanful of seniors to arrive. Then she'd saunter out to see which of her friends had come that day and whether any had brought doggie treats. As each group entered the center and individuals took their places at their favorite tables, Sandy would make the rounds. She'd stop to say hello to the new arrivals and give them one of her million-dollar smiles.

Then it was back to the lobby for Sandy until breakfast was served. That's when she'd help out the maintenance guy by clearing away the bits of food that always hit the floor. Plus Sandy had learned that, if she waited long enough, someone would slip a bit of meat or a scrap of biscuit to her under the table, even though it was against the rules.

Sandy may have been slow moving, but she was still able to pull the occasional caper. One time she discovered a plateful of doughnuts in the executive director's office. Could she help it if someone left such a delightful treat within reach? She probably should have gotten credit for leaving the plate spotless — on the floor, but spotless. At first we weren't sure who had swiped the doughnuts, and I tried to defend my dog against the allegations. But then we found her, four-paws-up, asleep in a corner, with a smile on her face and sugar glaze around her mouth. Guilty as charged.

Her stomach may have motivated Sandy's capers, but sometimes her tendency to steal food was actually helpful. One day as I worked in my office, Sandy trotted through the doorway with a small milk carton clenched in her teeth. She let it drop to the floor, and out fell several scraps of hardened meat. Immediately Sandy plopped down, intending to enjoy the bounty.

No sooner did Sandy spill her treasure on the floor than the center's nurse appeared. She'd followed Sandy and watched what she'd done. The story the nurse told amazed me. One of our seniors, Bertie, was in the habit of saving bits of her lunch to take home in empty milk cartons. That wouldn't have been a problem, except that Bertie would forget and let the food stay in her purse for days or even weeks. Then she'd find it, eat it, and end up very sick. This time, Bertie had saved some pork steak, which had been served a week earlier. As Sandy had made her rounds under the lunch-room table, she'd happened upon Bertie's purse and the delicious aroma of old meat. My dog's larcenous tendencies had gotten the better of her. She had grabbed the carton and run, followed closely by the nurse, who tattled on her. Fortunately for Sandy, I took the food away. Even for a dog, the scraps looked questionable.

I apologized profusely for Sandy's thievery, but the nurse stopped me cold. "It's okay," she said. "Sandy might've saved Bertie from serious illness. Imagine if, in this hot weather, Bertie had found that week-old pork steak and eaten it. She could have become violently ill. Sandy actually did a good thing by stealing it." I'd like to believe that Sandy's motives were pure, but I know better. She was exercising the old five-finger discount, taking what she wanted without payment or permission, but I credit her with saving Bertie's life.

She's Our Dog Too

Eventually, age began to take a toll on Sandy, and she developed fatty tumors at all her leg joints. My veterinarian assured me that the tumors were not dangerous but said they would eventually grow so big that walking would become uncomfortable. Surgery to remove the tumors would cost $235. That seemed reasonable. But for a single mom working for a struggling not-for-profit, that amount of money was monumental. The surgery would have to wait.

Most of the seniors had become so attached to my dog that they regarded her as their own. I hadn't mentioned Sandy's problem to anyone at the center, but Earl noticed the tumors and asked me about them. Earl was always the first to take note of anything new. He had physical disabilities, but his mind was still sharp, even if his leg problems made walking difficult. Unlike many of the participants, Earl had a spouse still living. She helped him with grooming, so Earl always looked sharp and alert — two qualities that were rare at the senior center. Since Earl had a special love for Sandy, I told him about the vet's diagnosis. "Some day I'll get them removed but I just can't do it now," I said to him.

That afternoon, Earl appeared in my office doorway along with a female staff member. Earl was glowing with what he considered a brilliant idea. "Why don't we start a fund for Sandy and raise money for her surgery? After all, she's our dog too!" The staff member echoed Earl's sentiments. "Let's ask the boss. It would be good for all of us," she said.

I was sure that our boss would be appalled. Yes, I was struggling financially, but compared to these senior citizens, I was practically rolling in cash. I thanked Earl for his kind suggestion but didn't mention it to anyone. Even so, the next day my boss came into my office and told me to make a thermometer-style donations chart for the lunchroom wall.

"A donations chart?" I asked. "What are we collecting for?"

She explained that Earl had come to her with his idea about raising money for Sandy's surgery. "Most of these people haven't felt needed for a long time," she said. "This will give them a purpose, a project. Something to think about besides their own problems. It'll take a long time to raise the money, but it's not a life-or-death issue for Sandy. So get that chart made, and let's see what happens."

Sandy's Fund-Raiser

I drew a large thermometer on a poster and displayed it on the lunchroom wall. Almost every morning as I'd walk to the kitchen for coffee, one or more of the seniors would give me a donation for the object of their affection and mine. Earl, or one of the other participants, would hold my hand in both of his before leaving behind a few warm coins. As I'd return from refilling my coffee cup and head for my office, I'd look at the collection of copper coins in my hand and grin. Most mornings, the contributions averaged about thirteen pennies. Regardless of the size of the donation, my fellow employees and I always made a huge fuss over the amount.

On the donation thermometer, I kept track of the money contributed. That way, the seniors could watch as the total grew. Once a week, I'd raise the red line on the thermometer ever so slightly, and we'd all cheer as though, instead of trickling in painfully slowly, the money were stacking up fast.

Then two things happened. First, someone who did not work at or attend the center heard about the project and sent a sizable donation. And second, someone at work contacted my vet and told him that the seniors were collecting money for Sandy's surgery. The story must have touched the vet's heart, because he said he'd match the donations. If they could raise half the price, he'd take that as full payment.

Sandy's Gift

Finally Sandy's surgery took place. I'd arranged to stay home with her afterward, since she needed to remain quiet for a few days following the procedure. When her week of recovery was over, Sandy made her triumphant return to the center with a new spring in her step, a wag in her tail, and the ever-present smile on her face. She wore a T-shirt designed to protect her stitches. Her arrival was that of a war hero returning from battle. If the seniors could have managed it, they would have raised her on their shoulders and carried her into the center. The truth was, they were the real heroes.

I don't know if Sandy understood what those sweet old folks did for her, but she knew for sure she was loved. It took a few more days of recovery, but soon her steps were quicker and her tail wagged a little more convincingly as she made her way through the recreation room, greeting her loyal fans. The seniors had dug deep into their nearly empty pockets and come up with a few pennies a day for an old gray dog who needed their help.

As for me, I couldn't help but choke up at the thought of how they loved her, and me. Without a doubt, having Sandy there and sharing her with these fine people was a far better work-related benefit than I could get elsewhere. When I started the job, the center had been without a fiscal officer for months and desperately needed someone to get the books back into shape. My intention had been to stay one year, just long enough to get them over the hump. I had never envisioned staying five years. But then, I also hadn't known that I'd be able to have Sandy with me, or that those seniors would work their way into my heart as they did.

In return for their love and attention, Sandy gave the seniors a smile and a warm greeting and let them forget their troubles for a while. She had more than enough love for everyone. She may have gone home with me each night, but for as long as she was my partner at the senior center, she was their dog too. Sandy was a working girl, but her work was a labor of love.

MEDITATION

With the gift of healing comes gratitude. When have you and a dog reciprocated by healing each other?

Miguel's Legacy

Rosanne Nordstrom, CHICAGO, ILLINOIS

Every morning, Monday through Friday, I take an eight-year-old girl, who likes to be called Princess, to school. At three o'clock I pick her up and we go to violin or piano lessons, math tutoring, and soccer or basketball practice. On weekends I watch her play sports. In between these activities, we hang out. I garden, and she digs for worms or hunts insects. We color drawings in books, using crayons and colored pencils. We practice our violins and do homework. Sometimes Princess helps me cook.

My days are like those of any mother, aunt, or grandmother with an eight-year-old in her life. I, however, am sixty and never wanted or had children of my own. I am not bound to Princess by blood or a legal relationship. Sometimes she calls me her fairy grandmother. I gained this title by cooperating with a big black Newfoundland–Labrador retriever and a needy eight-year-old boy I will call Paco.

I might have maintained my childfree state for a lifetime, except that, three years after our first dog died, I decided that my husband, Roger, missed living with a dog. Off I went to a no-kill shelter and returned with a three-month-old pup who was more Newfoundland, or Newf, than Labrador. He had a barely healed broken hip that was badly set but couldn't be rebroken and set correctly, and yet I wanted him anyway.

At the shelter, Miguel was one of the few dogs who didn't bark or carry on as I walked down the aisle. He sat up straight at the very front of his crate. He remained still except for the very end of his tail, which gave a little wag. He had an expectant look about him that seemed to say, "Do you recognize me? I'm the one you want." When the shelter caretaker talked to me, she mentioned that Miguel appeared lame but also told me that the dog was part Newf. That did it for me. I'd met my first Newf a decade earlier, and I loved the breed. I'd known at first glance that this black puppy was the one I wanted to bring home. That he was part Newf made him even more special.

I don't know how feeding was handled at the shelter, but the new puppy wasn't skilled at eating from a dog dish. Maybe he thought food in a big metal bowl was just another game or toy. The first time Roger and I watched him slap and roll his dish around the kitchen floor, taking an occasional break to eat, I burst out laughing and said, "He reminds me of that bear cub we saw at Lincoln Park Zoo, the one they named Miguel." For the messy eater in our home, Miguel felt like the right name.

Miguel Attracts the Children

After his housebreaking was complete, we usually took Miguel for three walks a day. Because our condo was half a block away from a public elementary school, and because Miguel was big and calm, he soon had an abundance of children as his friends. One morning in late May, Miguel and I met four boys who walked a few blocks with us. All of them, they soon told me, were in second grade. Like almost all the other kids in the neighborhood, they were black and approached us with caution. Three of them were neatly dressed in slacks with tucked-in shirts. One of the boys asked, "Hey, lady, is that your dog? Does he bite?"

I always gave the same answer to the children when they asked this question: "This is Miguel. He's friendly. He'd never bite you."

Sadly, most of those children's experiences with dogs had been with the ones they called bad, ones that snarled or bit. Once assured that Miguel was good, they swarmed around us. I didn't mind talking to them about him: what he ate (everything, even lettuce and grapefruit), how big he was (almost a hundred pounds), and where he slept (in our room on his own dog bed).

Miguel liked to chew. The best part of his afternoon walk was the stop we made at a park. It was always littered with tree branches, which Miguel picked up, threw into the air and caught, shook, and then settled down to tear into pieces with his teeth. I always sat on the sandbox and watched his play, partly to make sure he didn't choke and partly because I enjoyed the enthusiasm Miguel brought to the task.

As we walked and I talked with the four boys that day, all of a sudden Miguel flew into a bush and came out with a tennis ball in his mouth. A university tennis court about four blocks away supplied the neighborhood with many balls. Miguel delighted in finding them to bring home. He chased the balls throughout our apartment or chewed them until he could pop the ball like a kid with noisy gum. Tennis ball popping was his indoor version of chewing tree branches.

Because of Miguel's tennis ball find, one of the boys asked how many balls Miguel had at home. "The last time I counted, there were more than seventy," I replied.

"No way. That's too many. Can we see them?"

Now, twenty years later, I can look back and see that this was the moment when, if I'd stayed true to form, I would have denied the boys' request. It wasn't the first time a group of children had walked with us. Sometimes there were more than I could easily count. Nor was this the first request a child had made to visit Miguel in his house. The vision of an unending parade of children ringing the bell to play with Miguel always made me answer, "Not today."

My house and my life would have remained free of children had I said no. But this time I said, "Sure, you can come in until we hear the first school bell ring." Even today, remembering the ease with which those words flew out of my mouth astounds me, and I have no explanation for breaking my no-children-allowed rule that day.

At home, Miguel enjoyed the boys' company, and this group was especially exciting for him. They found every last ball in the toy box and were soon rolling or tossing them for Miguel to catch. I sat on the couch, stunned by their energy, movement, and noise. I began to listen carefully for the school bell and noticed that one of the boys had left the frenzied play and wandered into the sunporch. He sat down and began paging through an oversized art book I'd left on the wicker coffee table.

I kept an eye on Miguel and company but also watched the loner. He was the smallest of the boys and the worst dressed and groomed. He wore dirty black pants that were way too big and an aqua-blue shirt with black stripes that wasn't tucked in; it was missing a couple buttons. He had beautiful, large, dark brown eyes outlined by long, thick lashes. His smile was huge, and a dimple appeared in each cheek when he grinned. He was as good-looking as any young boy I'd ever seen. He looked through my book of R. C. Gorman lithographs as if he were quite interested. Young boys who played with my dog were what I had expected. That one of them would be attracted to a big book, even one with pictures, surprised me.

At last, the school bell rang. The boys left. Miguel sat panting on the dining room floor. I went to the kitchen for a cup of coffee and continued with my day.

Miguel's Complicated New Friend

More and more often, as the days passed, my doorbell rang. Hearing it, Miguel would race to the sunporch, where he could see the front door from our first-floor windows. Almost always the doorbell ringer was Paco with the ragged clothing and beautiful eyes, the boy I had suspected was not all that interested in art books. In later years, my suspicions were confirmed when Paco reminisced about his first times in our house. He said, "You guys had so many books, more than I ever saw at school. I knew you had to be rich." Books were a symbol of a better life to Paco, but he never read more than he had to.

Each time Paco arrived at my doorstep and rang the buzzer, Miguel would bark and run from the sunporch to the doorbell intercom and back to the front of the house. It was as if he were trying to reassure the young caller. "Don't worry. I'm working on her. Just keep ringing that bell."

More and more often, I buzzed Paco inside. But there were times when I didn't feel like watching Miguel and Paco race around the apartment. At those times, when Miguel realized that I wasn't accepting any company, he'd heave himself down in front of me, give a long sigh, and look as if I'd disappointed him. And I'd say, "This apartment is huge. Why don't you take your big sighs and soulful looks to another room?"

An unanswered door never kept Paco away for long. He was always clear about his reason for persisting. "I've been watching you and Roger walk Miguel. My grams died last year. I know I need someone to take care of me. I like the way you treat Miguel. You walk him a lot and pet him. You talk nice to him, and he sure doesn't look hungry. I'm hoping you'll treat me as good."

Over the course of his visits, Paco talked about his life. He had a mother and three aunts: one who lived in the building next to ours, and two who shared an apartment around the corner. Although he lived with his mother, he spent more time with his aunts than at home.

Paco sometimes complained that I spent too much time with Miguel and talked to him way too much, which was, in Paco's opinion, "real stupid if you expect the dog to answer." Even so, when Paco was alone with Miguel, he threw balls for the dog to retrieve. They played endless games of tug-of-war with old socks.

The game I found strangest was one he called playing dead. For Miguel, it was a matter of stretching out on the floor to rest. Then Paco would get down on the floor, stretch out, close his eyes, and yell, "Look, Rosie, I'm dead." If one of the purposes of play is to ready a child for more grown-up tasks, as when they cook on

a toy stove or build with blocks, then Paco seemed to be preparing for his more grown-up days by playing dead. Ultimately his dire predictions of what to expect from a childhood like his came true: when he was nearly sixteen, a friend of his was shot and killed in a drug deal gone bad.

Death also figured in Paco's conversations with me about Miguel. "Who will take care of Miguel if you die? What will you do if Miguel dies? Will you cry?" These conversations left me feeling uneasy. Miguel was getting older, and of course, dying is the inevitable end for all of us, but I didn't want to dwell on my dog's passing. Nor did I want to think about why Paco would segue into how I would react to his dying. I had the feeling that I was part of something I didn't understand, and that I was in way over my head.

Rosanne's Miguel

When Paco wasn't talking about death, he was fun to be with. My husband, Roger, enjoyed spending time with Paco too. They walked Miguel together, played basketball, washed the car, and played chess.

After a year of day visits, Paco decided it was time to spend nights with us. We put him to bed in the room next to ours. Often during the night, Paco would sneak into our room and join Miguel on his bed. Miguel was good about sharing.

A New Life

Two years after meeting Paco, Roger and I moved from our Hyde Park condo on Chicago's South Side to a house on the far north side of the city. The two places were forty-five minutes apart on the fastest route by car; public transportation took at least an hour and a half. As a ten-year-old child, Paco had to follow whatever rules his mother or aunts decreed. Thinking about making arrangements to spend time with Paco once we were separated by such a long distance left me feeling bone tired. Before leaving for our new home, we asked Paco's mother if we could pick up the boy after school on Fridays to spend the weekend with us. She said it would be okay. Week after week, on Fridays, Paco ran from his school's door to my waiting car, and off we drove to be together in our new home.

Life in our new house was good. Miguel and I took daily walks to the lakefront. Now we had both a deck and a backyard, which Miguel loved as long as I went out there with him, since he wanted to be wherever I was. The winter after we moved, there were several snowstorms. When Paco visited, he enjoyed having Roger or me bury him under a huge mound of snow so that Miguel could dig him out. Miguel enjoyed doing so, and I noted that Paco had moved on from games of death to ones of rescue.

Miguel lived for a little less than a year at the new house. He died of complications of crippling from severe arthritis caused by the early break in his hip. I dreaded giving the news to Paco, whose first question was the one I expected: "Did you cry?"

"No, but Roger did, and both of us were with Miguel when he died."

"So you didn't really love Miguel?"

"Oh, Paco."

That afternoon I didn't care to explain that I felt as if I'd been beaten up and left for dead. Flickering around my grief were bursts of anger. Miguel had lived a good life, but it might have been longer if, when his hip had been broken, it had been taken care of immediately. Someone hadn't been paying attention or hadn't thought caring for Miguel was worth the effort, time, and money that a trip to the vet would have entailed.

Often, I slipped from anger about the pain Miguel had endured to compassion for Paco. In the sad weeks after Miguel's death, I came closer and closer to being willing to commit fully to the youngster. Had it been possible for Miguel to describe either Roger or me, I think he'd have said, "They're both strong. They are loyal. They're kind and gentle." To that, I would add that both of us are intelligent. Roger is a rock of dependability. I have been blessed with an endless supply of words. And we are incredibly stubborn. We needed and constantly used all these qualities in the years after Miguel's death, as Roger and I fought hard to give Paco the life he wanted.

Paco's New Home

In the middle of seventh grade, Paco decided to move into our house and live there full-time. He told one of his aunts what he wanted, and she got his school records transferred to the public school near our house. Besides helping Paco with his nightly homework and sports, we began going to physicians, dentists, orthodontists, and therapists. We had many meetings with school principals and teachers. Although Roger and I never had a legal relationship with Paco, when we took him to professionals we'd ask that they use their skills to help, and we promised to support their efforts and to pay in full.

Paco's adolescence was what might be expected of any child born into terrible poverty on Chicago's South Side. Roger and I became familiar with the juvenile court system, probation terms, and drug counseling. Paco and I spent hours and hours with home schooling. We also continued fun activities and vacation trips. When our lives felt overwhelming, as they often did, I would recall the chain of events that began on the day I saw Miguel, an adorable black puppy at a shelter, and how this dog had led me to Paco.

As Paco traveled through his twenties, I sometimes wished out loud to him that his life had taken a more traditional and less stressful route. His answer? "But Rosie, I'm not dead. And I'm not in prison."

By 2009, two of Paco's close family members were incarcerated. More of Paco's boyhood friends than I can keep track of have been killed by gunfire in gang- and drug-related activities.

A Sunday Soccer Game

The most striking difference between Paco at eight years of age and his daughter, Princess, who is that age now, is that Princess is blessed with a mother who has nurtured her in every way.

One Sunday afternoon, I took Princess to her soccer game. Many people were watching the games. As soon as she and I neared the soccer field, I noticed a Newf sitting with his people. He was huge, even for the breed. I stopped and talked to the dog before moving on to where Princess and her team waited to play. In a while, Paco joined me to watch his daughter. Back at my house, he immediately asked, "Hey, Rosie, did you see the Newf?"

Before I could answer, Princess said, "Yeah, Rose stopped to pet the dog. She talked to him too. I was afraid she'd be late for my game." Paco smiled. I thought to myself, There is no way Princess could begin to imagine what her dad remembers when he sees a

Newf. She wouldn't understand that a Newf reminds her dad of a time when he watched an apparently healthy, happy dog interact with two grown-ups and envied the dog.

As time passed, I grew to like the idea that I became a person who made a firm commitment to a child who needed me and helped him grow up strong and happy with his life. I'm proud of the part I've played in helping Princess to live an ordinary life with none of the experiences that her father barely survived. I'm sure Paco would join me wholeheartedly in saying, "Thank you, Miguel, for beginning this long, many-chaptered story."

MEDITATION

Rosanne, Roger, Paco, and Miguel formed a vortex of love that transformed and united them as a family. Could the loyalty and commitment of a dog inspire you to share your resources with those who need them?

Growing Up Dog Weird

Susan Hartzler, NORTHRIDGE, CALIFORNIA

My childhood dog Siesta taught me all about love. She was supposed to be a full-bred Chihuahua, but my parents speculated that she was most likely a terrier mix. Whatever she was, that small gray dog with dark brown, soulful eyes looked as if she had stepped in white paint and used the tips of her feet to brush streaks on her tail and chest.

Because of my bond with this funny-looking little dog so early in life, I have always felt most comfortable with a canine by my side. I realize now that my family was embarrassed about my intense attachment to that dog. But right or wrong, I was (and still am) dog weird.

Being dog weird is not so strange considering I'm in excellent company. The goddess Diana, from Roman mythology, shared my love and reverence for the canine spirit. Diana is also found in Greek mythology as Artemis, goddess of the moon, the heavenly light that illuminates the darkness, who ruled the wilderness, the untamed frontiers of nature. Diana was powerful and complex and was celebrated as the goddess of childbirth, women, song, dance, and animals. It's interesting that the lunar goddess loved dogs, who were known to howl at the moon. In fact, dogs were among Diana's most sacred animals. Diana, also known as goddess of the hunt, is portrayed in images and statues as having long blonde hair and wearing flowing robes on her tall and slender body. She carries a bow and arrow and is accompanied by her faithful dogs and a strong young stag.

When I picture Diana with her dogs, I am immediately transported to my childhood in the suburbs of Los Angeles, and to my Siesta. She got her name because that was the only Spanish word my father knew, and he thought it was an ironic name for the active puppy.

The instant she joined our family, I never wanted to go anywhere without her. When I wasn't with her, I missed her fur's nutty aroma and her tiny feet that smelled like corn chips. She was supposed to be the family pet, but everyone knew Siesta was my dog. She slept with me. She followed me everywhere. I carried her around in my backpack. She drank from my Betsy Wetsy doll's baby bottle and ate doughnuts and bologna while sitting in a high chair.

That wire-haired, goofy-looking dog meant everything to me. I felt lost without her. I pushed her in a toy baby carriage, secretly fed her scraps from the dinner table, and cuddled with her all night. I even knit a scarf and a winter hat, with holes for her pointy ears, for Siesta to wear when it was chilly outside.

Christmas Stealth

One cold December morning when I was about six, I went on a mission to celebrate Christmas with Siesta in my own way. I snuck into my mom's forbidden private dresser drawer. I had been warned not to touch Mom's things and never to go near her dresser. But I had seen in it the bewitching bottles and jars of sweet-smelling potions and lotions. That day, I just couldn't help myself. When I was certain Mom was in the kitchen, I carefully pulled open the drawer and searched through her makeup. Knowing exactly what I was looking for, I passed up the bottles of

Clinique moisturizer that I so badly wanted to open. I had to hurry. At the very back of the drawer, I found Mom's bright red lipstick in its sleek silver case. Grabbing it, I ran outside as fast as I could. Bringing my little dog with me to our personal Eden, I entered the best space in our home — our backyard. There, anything was possible.

This vast half acre, more like a park than a yard, provided a refuge in which to make my own adventures, where all I needed was my imagination and my dog. Ivy draped down the fence around the space where I created my wonderland. In this space stood a mature walnut tree that was perfect for climbing, a young lemon tree that bore the juiciest and tartest lemons, and two giant cypress trees occupied by squirrels who drove Siesta wild as they played hide-and-seek. My backyard transformed into an enchanted forest of lush alpine meadows where Siesta and I roamed freely through the fierce mists.

There, I pretended we were a deer family. My ten-pound dog took the role of baby fawn, and I was her mother doe. I knew from watching nature shows and reading about deer families that a doe takes intense care of her fawn and teaches her how to survive in the world. I have been drawn to the relationship, the bond, the beauty, and the strength of these animals for as long as I remember.

Creating Rudolph

When I first learned the story of Rudolph and how he saved Christmas, he, not Santa, became my hero. That day near Christmas when I stole my mother's lipstick, Siesta and I were heroes with no one to bother us except Mother Nature. The first step to becoming the legendary Rudolph, Santa's most famous reindeer, was for me to paint our noses red. Siesta's first. I carefully held her snout and smeared red lipstick onto her entire black nose. It was not easy. Lipstick is not meant to cover a doggie's wet nose. On top of that, a squirrel bolted across our yard when I was only halfway through the job. Siesta exploded out of my arms to give chase and broke off the lipstick's tip.

I picked up the broken piece now covered in grass and jammed it back into the tube. I applied red and bits of grass to my nose. Once in character, Siesta and I trotted around the yard. Under sunny skies, we were magically transformed into two little Rudolphs.

Siesta gave me her full attention for the rest of that day as I sang my favorite Christmas song, "Rudolph the Red-Nosed Reindeer." She looked up at me lovingly as she trotted by my side along the perimeter of the yard. Nothing in the world mattered except the two of us. I imagined we were in Santa's stable at the North Pole. Outside the magical toy shop, little green elves readied for the big night when dreams would come true for all the good little boys and girls around the world.

The sleigh was loaded, and Santa got on board. We were about to take off, rounding the corners of the yard, running faster

Susan's Siesta

and faster. I was in the lead with Siesta at my feet, her little legs spreading out as far as they could go. Our red noses were brighter than the sun. My strides started to lengthen. I leapt high in the air. The wind blew against my face. I heard Santa: "What do you have on your face? Is that lipstick? Is that *my* lipstick on the dog?"

Galloping away from my mom, who had broken the spell, I tried to head off Siesta.

"Susan Frances, I'm speaking to you."

"Oh no, she's using my middle name," I thought.

"Mom, we're about to take off. Santa needs us to guide his sleigh or else all the good children won't get their presents."

"If you don't come here right now, Santa's not going to bring you any presents, young lady. In fact, I have a mind to send you away to the North Pole. All by yourself." She grabbed my hand and dragged me into the house.

With or without a red nose, I continued to use my imagination to play deer family with Siesta. I envisioned her as a golden fawn with white spots; her big pointy ears made her resemble a miniature deer in the wild. Other people remarked that she looked like a giant rat.

Rudolph Goes to School One Day

It wasn't possible to spend every moment playing with Siesta. I had to leave her all day while I was at school, and it seemed like cruel punishment, even though I liked my first grade teacher, Mrs. Berger. She was a nice-looking woman with short, dark, stylish hair and bangs that framed her brown, caring eyes. She wore matching sweater sets and skirts along with flesh-toned stockings that made a swishing sound as she passed by our desks. I don't remember ever hearing her raise her voice, but she always managed to keep the class in line.

Mrs. Berger smelled like my all-time favorite flower, lily of the valley, whose little white blossoms reminded me of bells. She was ladylike and intelligent and explained to us everything there was to know in the entire world. One day, she asked us to draw a picture of what we would like to be when we grew up.

My classmates drew pictures of astronauts and actresses, pilots and zookeepers. As each student brought his or her drawing to the front of the room, Mrs. Berger smiled with delight.

Then it was my turn. I wore my ginger-colored peasant dress with my favorite desert boots. My mom had begged me not to wear those shoes with dresses, but I loved them. They were my absolute favorites — dark brown, rubber-soled, suede booties that came to my ankles, accented by my white socks.

I stood up confidently, holding in my hand the picture I had drawn. I walked to the front of the room, turned the drawing around, and held it high above my head. I smiled as I looked around. My picture was the best of all, and I knew it.

Wearing her lemon sweater set and resting her hands in her lap, Mrs. Berger gazed at my drawing. Her smile froze like those of the mannequins I saw when I had to endure shopping excursions with my mom. I had drawn a reindeer who looked like the ones Siesta and I pretended to be.

I scanned the classroom. My friends laughed and pointed at me, and my face flushed red in embarrassment. Quickly I brought the picture down. Could I have been mistaken to draw the reindeer? My face turned sour. My eyes flashed anger at the kids I thought were my friends. My stomach ached, making flip-flops as I stood there. I didn't know what to do next.

Mrs. Berger didn't seem to know what to say about my drawing of Rudolph. "I see you chose Rudolph because he saved Christmas with his red nose," she said, trying her best to give me a graceful way out.

"No, I chose Rudolph because I like him," I shouted at her. I knew not to admit that I liked to pretend my little dog was the fabled Christmas reindeer.

"Okay, Susie, we'll let someone else have a turn." She motioned for me to sit down. I stomped back to my seat, defeated but determined that when I grew up I would show them all. I would become a reindeer one day.

Later that year, for our Christmas pageant, I sang "Rudolph the Red-Nosed Reindeer" while my dad accompanied me on the piano. The entire school had come to the auditorium for the annual holiday assembly. I was more excited that my dad was there than nervous about performing in front of about five hundred kids. Besides, I had a naturally beautiful singing voice.

As I belted out the words, I looked down at my feet. My brown desert boots turned into little reindeer hoofs, and the stark white tiles of the floor transformed into snowbanks. I closed my eyes and felt myself flying at remarkable speeds, the cold air and snow bothering me not one bit. I felt the pull of the sleigh as we landed on rooftops. Santa slid down chimneys, leaving presents for all of the world's good little boys and girls. When I finished and the applause began, I opened my eyes. I took a bow and smiled. I had done the impossible. For just one moment, I had become Rudolph.

The next day, I jumped out of bed with Siesta and ran out to our backyard as fast as I could. Setting her down on the grass wet with morning dew, I motioned for her to trot alongside me. I wanted Siesta to feel the sensation I had felt the night before when I sang at my school. Now I knew it didn't have to do with painting our noses or with anything else on the outside. The magic was on the inside.

As we rounded the corner of the yard, I whispered to my little dog: "Close your eyes. Feel the pull of the sleigh. Hear Santa's voice." When I looked at her, Siesta's black nose was in the air. Her eyes were closed. And I could swear she had a smile on her face.

MEDITATION

What are your favorite childhood memories with dogs?
How "dog weird" are you?

Remembering Buster Dawn

Karen Dawn, PACIFIC PALISADES, CALIFORNIA

As Thanksgiving approached last year, neighbors asked if I would be adopting turkeys again. I thought of last year's turkeys lined up at the front gate with my dogs, Paula Pitbull and Buster — an unlikely foursome greeting people who passed by on their way to the bluff to watch the sunset. I thought of Buster's patience when the turkey named Bruce, later renamed Brucilla after he laid an egg, usurped Buster's bed on the porch. Mostly I thought that this year Buster would not be here to guard the turkeys. It would be my first holiday season in twelve years without Buster Dawn.

Buster came to me in November 1997, a tiny puppy whom I adopted from New York's North Shore Animal League. I wasn't yet involved in animal advocacy, for which Buster later became my muse, so I didn't know then that I should have adopted an older dog because puppies always get homes — and because I would have liked to keep my rugs, furniture, and shoe collection intact.

All the puppies at the shelter were adorable, and I played with many before noticing the little tiger-striped brindle boy in the corner — probably a pit bull mix. While the other puppies had squirmed when I picked them up, curious about everything around them, Buster had focused on my face and started to lick it. In my favorite photo of him, he attacks my cheek with his tongue as I throw back my head in laughter. The photo was taken ten years after that first day at the shelter — nothing had changed.

For all those years, Buster's daily exfoliation treatment was at the center of my skin care regime. What will become of my complexion now that he is gone?

On our first Thanksgiving together, I carried Buster to a friend's house in a shoebox. The rescue folks had told me he would eventually grow to be about thirty-five pounds. Ha! Apparently they gave him the same misinformation: years later, he would still regularly attempt to sit in my lap when we were out together at cafés. All seventy-five pounds of him. Usually he would leave his back legs on the ground and sling his top half over me — head high enough to lick my face. But occasionally, perhaps when I was having a fat day, he would decide that my lap looked big enough for all of him. When people would look at us and start laughing, he would open his mouth in a happy little grin, as if to say, "Isn't this great, Mom?"

Once Buster had had all his shots and was ready for New York pavements, we took our first walk together. It was Christmas. I strolled the Soho streets with my beautiful brindle puppy, awed that for once I was not walking alone. A few weeks later we wandered over to the East Village, and I called my friend Eric to ask him to come and grab a coffee with me, as we were right on his corner. His response: "Oh, Karen, I just love that you are a 'we' now."

Forming a Family

Yes, Buster changed me to we. Nights spent in my apartment watching television had always been lonely; with Buster they were cozy and fun. And I think Buster opened my heart and made it possible for Jim to enter a year later. The day Jim and I first met, we had lunch at Balthazar; and when he dropped me back at my apartment, he met Buster and Paula, Buster's newly adopted sister. Buster immediately suggested a ball game, and Jim obliged.

When Jim stopped by to pick me up for dinner that night, I was running late and asked if he would mind waiting in the little bookstore across the street. He said, "Sure. Or do the dogs need walking?" My heart almost burst — I had found my canine kids a wonderful daddy. Buster led Jim on our usual walk around Soho. Soon we all moved to Pacific Palisades in California and became a family.

We were a close family. Jim insisted that we never go on family holidays anywhere we couldn't take the dogs. Once he had heard Buster's fantastic rendition of "Happy Birthday," he couldn't bear a birthday without it. Buster had quite a voice: what he lacked in tone he made up for in gusto.

Thanksgivings were always spent at home. I would cook for days and then invite vegan friends to share the feast — plenty of Wild Turkey (bourbon!) and "veganized" versions of classic dishes. Buster loved sweet potatoes. I once made the mistake of leaving a bowl of them on the lower shelf of our serving trolley, and although the boy had beautiful manners and would never grab food off a table, he clearly thought the treat on this low-hanging bough had been left there for him. Thank heavens my guests were all animal lovers. They cackled when they saw Buster wolfing down our sweet potatoes and were happy to dig into the dish once I had skimmed Buster's personal gravy off the top.

One Christmas, we drove to Mexico and rented a guesthouse. Its front patio and another patio leading to the main house were both attached to a landing above stairs that led down to the street. In the main house, Chumaka and Amiga, a rottweiler mix and a coyote mix, lived with their humans. As we brought stuff up from the car to our Christmas abode, Chumaka and Amiga guarded the landing like customs officers inspecting imports. Everything passed muster except for Paula and Buster.

The canine guards at first refused to let our guys beyond the landing, but Buster somehow slipped past the sentinels into our guesthouse. A moment later he emerged, carrying a new dog toy that Jim had put under the Christmas tree. He slunk onto the landing, darted over to Chumaka and Amiga's patio, dropped the toy, and darted back. Chumaka and Amiga gave up their post to check out the peace offering. For the next week we were a pack of six: walks to the beach involved all four dogs — the peacemaking mutt, the rottweiler mix, the coyote mix, and the pit bull. Nobody fracked with us!

Paula recently reminded me of Buster's sweet gift-giving gesture. The two of them had always been inseparable, but in the last few weeks of Buster's life, as he lost the use of his back legs, he was no longer able to play with Paula. And I suspect she may have been jealous, as I was no longer able to give both dogs equal attention; Buster needed to be carried, constantly cleaned, and generally nursed. Paula gave the weakening Buster a wide berth. But her grief after we let her explore his lifeless body was undeniable. After we placed Buster in his grave, she lay beside it for hours with her paws hanging over. She brought a toy and dropped it in on top of him. Unsure the move had been intentional, I gave it back to her. She dropped it in again. We buried her sweet offering with our sweet boy.

Buster and *Battlestar*

In those last few weeks of Buster's life, as I prepared to face an almost unfathomable loss, I reflected deeply on my relationship with my dog. It so happened that the day before I learned of Buster's inoperable spinal tumor, I had started watching the recently remade *Battlestar Galactica* series. (If you're a *Battlestar* fan, you will have noticed the series reference above: my use of the word *fracked*.) In the last month of Buster's life, we spent every night on the couch together in front of the television watching all four seasons of the series. I am such a fan of the show that I could go on about it for the next few pages. But I will do my best to share just enough to explain how its message, absorbed over the weeks in which I said good-bye to Buster Dawn, profoundly affected my thinking about our relationship — and then my wider thinking about relationships between species.

In *Battlestar Galactica*, the humans are at war with the Cylons. The Cylons were created by humans to be robot slaves. They developed consciousness, rebelled, and managed to design humanlike bodies for themselves and become indistinguishable from humans. While that sounds like a standard sci-fi horror setup, there is a fundamental twist: the Cylons truly are indistinguishable from humans. While the humans call the Cylons "toasters" and tell themselves that Cylons are machines that don't feel pain and don't have emotions, the viewer sees the Cylons exhibiting pain and emotions, including love and loyalty. It becomes clear to the viewer that, regardless of their origin, the Cylons in humanlike bodies are no less sentient than humans. Yet we see waterboarding scenes in which human characters that we have come to love treat the Cylons with unconscionable cruelty, justifying the torture because the victims are not human. In short, we see the age-old pattern of the way we let ourselves treat "the other."

A fascinating recurring phenomenon on the show is each human's reaction, the self-judgment, when she (or he) finds she has fallen in love with a Cylon. The individual humans have internalized society's message that there is something wrong with that love.

And so I started to look at my love for Buster. I have been blessed with much love in my life, including a ten-year relationship with Jim, Buster's human daddy, who is still a friend I adore.

But in truth, I have never loved anybody as dearly as I loved Buster. I write these words knowing that we aren't supposed to feel this way, and that other people may assume that I find relationships with human beings hard and so settled on a lesser relationship with a dog.

But was it lesser? Who has a human who howls down the house whenever he or she gets home from work? And what human could make my heart light up just by walking into the room? And that was every single time Buster walked in, no matter how many times a day. For me, the intellectual conversations about books and films that a human might offer — and not all do — cannot outweigh the joyful camaraderie of a dog on walks along the bluff, or the comfort of a trusting head on my lap as I curl up to read a good book or to watch humans fight "the other" on *Battlestar Galactica*. Meetings of the mind do not mean more than the meeting of souls that I felt when I looked into Buster's sweet eyes and he returned my loving gaze.

Karen and Buster Dawn

Before Buster, I had always felt there were limits to love. Only in the last weeks of his life did I learn what it was to care more for another than for myself. The last weeks of his life were some of the sweetest of mine. We spent almost every minute together, taking long sunset walks as I bathed in, drank in, the beauty of his companionship. When he lost the use of his back legs, we spent our days lying in the front yard under an umbrella together, me reading, him sleeping with his head on my thigh. After we headed inside, I would carry him out regularly to pee or would clean up after him when we didn't make it outside. I taught him to use a doggie wheelchair of sorts so that we could roll out onto the bluff for him to do his doggie business. As I packed up that wheelchair after his death, the smell of him on it, yes, even the smell of his pee, made me sob with yearning. I can still close my eyes, inhale, and smell Buster.

After twelve years of sleeping in my bed, Buster lost the ability to climb the stairs to it, and his bladder issues made it better for him to sleep in absorbent grass. So during the last week of his life, we slept outside together, I in a sleeping bag with my arms wrapped around him.

The Hardest Act of Love

I could have gone on like that forever with Buster. Caring for him was my joy. But when other dogs would run by our yard and Paula would dash down the hill for a fence fight, it was painful for me to watch Buster try to move and then only be able to bark from the spot we shared under the umbrella. His frustrated attempts to play ball were equally heartbreaking.

Ironically, those very attempts at normal, joyous, doggie behavior made the final decision torturous for me, as they showed that he was still full of life. But Jim asked me if, after twelve years of joy, I really wanted to wait till Buster had no interest in life, until he was utterly miserable, before letting him go? Did I want to wait until the pain had become unmanageable with medication and was piercing his sweet body?

No. So my love got the greatest test of all, as I chose to say good-bye to Buster before I was ready — I would probably never be ready — while it was still possible for his joyful life to end on a day of joy. Jim and I took Buster for a drive, his favorite thing to do, then took him home and lay with him in front of the fire. The vet came over late at night, once Buster was already sound asleep with his head on my lap. Buster died peacefully that way as my silent tears spilled onto my favorite face.

While I cried on the phone to a friend, he asked me to look for gratitude through the grief. He reminded me that not all people get to experience the kind of love I had with Buster. I was surprised by his words. I realize now that, like the humans on *Battlestar,* I had internalized the idea that our love, between species, was somehow lesser. I think I have finally let that go, and let go of the general societal notion that humans matter most — a belief that now seems as arbitrary as the idea that Americans matter most (if one happens to be American), or that people of a certain religion matter most.

Funny, ten years ago, seeing the plight of the animals and noticing how few would speak up for them, I vowed to give them my voice. Yet my message has been that, even if animals don't matter as much as humans, they still matter, and we must stop treating them as if they don't. Buster and *Battlestar* have made me rethink that message. Who says animals don't matter as much as humans? Buster did to me, and I choose to write, with pride, about how much he mattered.

I have now been through my first holiday season in twelve years without Buster Dawn. Jim moved out a year ago, so it was just us girls — me and Paula. It didn't feel much like a family. How we miss our boys. I love Paula, my little snuggle bunny and show-off, but when somebody once asked why Paula and not Buster is in all of my newspaper photos, I explained, "Buster is my heart, and I don't wear my heart on my sleeve."

Yes, Buster was my heart while he lived — but I didn't bury my heart with him when he died. It is more open and tender than ever. And I do manage to find the gratitude through the grief and to give thanks for the beautiful being who taught me about my capacity to love, completely. Buster's love is here even without the loving licks and heavenly howls that were its physical signs. And now, though our little family is no longer, I know there will one day be more love in my life, and more holidays with family — a family of humans, canines, turkeys, and any "others" who have come into my life and my open heart. That will be Buster's legacy.

MEDITATION

Has a special dog left a legacy for you and others to re-member? What is it?

TWO

Healing

Dogs are healers. They are enlightened. They seem to have figured out how to live beautifully so much better than we humans have. While we struggle to figure out why we were put here on Earth, all a dog wants is to love and be loved — a powerful lesson for us all.

— BERNARD S. SIEGEL, MD, "Dogs as Spiritual Messengers"

Lori and Beau Say to Disabled Veterans: "You've Got a Friend"

Lori Stevens, ROCKWALL, TEXAS

I've loved animals all my life. While I was in high school, my nickname was Sport, the name of my dog, because no one ever saw me without my red Irish setter. Sport was the constant companion of a young girl who needed a best friend — he kept me from feeling alone. I took him for long walks, and he was there for me 24-7. Sport inspired me to bring this kind of important companionship to others who need it. Life would take me down many paths, but eventually I would turn my love for dogs into a special way of serving disabled veterans, who have given so much to their country.

As my children got older, memories returned of my childhood experiences with the benefits of dog companionship. When my second child was in school, I began looking for a service dog organization I could work for. But raising a family and other obligations consumed nearly all my time, and twenty years passed before I followed up on my initial impulse to get involved with service dogs. I revisited that impulse when I went to the Texas Kennel Club dog show in downtown Dallas. This was a big dog show, and organizers had on hand a lot of information about training, rescue, obedience, and police dogs. I met two women from Plano, Texas, the only ones at the show doing service dog work.

At the booth they had set up for their nonprofit organization, Lone Star Assistance Dog Service, the women discussed whether they could continue their work given the hardships involved in raising funds and finding volunteers. This was the only nonprofit of its kind in the area. Lone Star's approach was to connect dogs and humans in ways that caused them to forge bonds of mutual love and respect. We talked for hours, and I begged the women not to close down their organization.

The women picked up on my enthusiasm and became excited too. Not a lot of people want to work for a nonprofit of this type and give it their undivided attention, time, and energy. It takes up to two years to train service dogs so that they fit into the human world. If an organization trains a hundred dogs, typically only twenty-five, or one out of four, will become certified as full-service dogs. After I realized the difference the Lone Star dogs could make in someone's life by helping him or her perform daily activities, I wanted to help too. I decided to join the organization.

One of the women, Ginny Bullock, taught me about clicker training and using positive reinforcement. She didn't jerk or pop the leash to correct a dog but instead built a positive relationship with the dog. This was what I'd had with Sport, so I immediately related to it. Ginny showed me that after becoming best friends with a person, a dog would do things out of love, rather than simply to avoid pain. This philosophy turned out to be a wonderful match for me.

Service Dog Beau

Volunteers with the Lone Star Assistance Dog Service found Beau, a black Lab, and his sister, Beth, running the streets west of Fort Worth. They tracked down the dogs' owners, who decided to give the dogs to the organization.

When I met Beau, one of the trainers was having a hard time with him because of Beau's overwhelming fear. Beau especially didn't like men coming up behind him. I asked Beau's trainer if I could take Beau home to work with. After I get a rescued dog, I choose a birthday for him or her, picking the holiday closest to the day when the dog was found. Beau's birthday became Saint Patrick's Day. I didn't know it at the time, but adopting him would turn out to be one of the best things that ever happened to me.

Beau's anxieties and skittishness made us wonder if he would ever become a service dog. The first week I had him, he escaped through a screened window and ran away. I thought maybe a loud noise, as from a tractor, might have scared him. We found out later that in addition to being a very shy dog, he was scared of the hot rods my husband and two teenage sons were assembling at the time. When the cars' loud noises frightened him, he would try to run off. One time, one of my son's friends unexpectedly came around a corner in our house and startled Beau. The terrified dog peed on the floor.

To relieve Beau's fearfulness, I started keeping him with me, and this constant companionship also enabled us to do therapy work together. We joined the Delta Society's Pet Partners program and began visiting nursing homes and hospitals. Using a home-study course from the Delta Society, I taught Beau how to do silly tricks. He could wave at people; he also could squat down and put his paws together to look as if he were saying his prayers. It soon became evident that Beau was a star at pet therapy.

On our trips to hospitals, Beau became a stress reliever not only for patients but also for the doctors and nurses. Seeing us coming down the hall, one of the doctors would yell, "Oh, my Beau." We would walk very quietly and peek in patients' doors to see if they wanted us to visit. It was an eye-opener for the staff to see that a dog could be such a positive influence in a hospital work environment.

Therapy dogs are required to be extra clean before entering hospitals and must take a bath each day before doing service work.

But bathtubs weren't the only places where Beau got wet. At times, long hospital visits can be stressful for a therapy dog, so on the way home after an especially long session, I would take Beau to the nearby lake for a swim. It was a reward and therapy for him to run in the water and retrieve sticks. It was wonderful for me to see him happy after he had made a difference in the hospital patients' day. The hospital work socialized Beau and made him less fearful. As he became better trained, I constantly tried new tasks with him.

In 1986, shortly after starting pet therapy at hospitals, I got a paying job with Texas Hearing and Service Dogs. We taught Beau how to do all the necessary hearing-service-dog behaviors, such as alerting a hearing-impaired person when someone is at the door, the phone is ringing, or the smoke alarm is buzzing. My boss said she noticed an increase in the organization's contributions at the end of the first year after Beau started giving demonstrations for companies during United Way campaigns.

Beau, David Letterman, and Animal Planet

In 2002, I stopped working with Texas Hearing and Service Dogs because my father was terminally ill. I started teaching family-pet obedience classes at the local PETCO in its parking lot. We would set up fifteen or twenty orange safety cones, and during class Beau would demonstrate basic obedience behaviors. Then he would sit on the tailgate of my truck until class was over. His reward was to retrieve all the orange safety cones. People driving by would slow down to watch him. We actually got many clients that way; they'd stop and talk to us about our cool dog.

We live in the country, and one night as I sat on the front porch with Beau I asked him, "What are we going to do now?" By then, my dad had passed and the kids were growing up. I had been playing on the computer before going outside that night, sending emails to people about how great Beau is and all the wonderful things he could do. On a whim, I sent an email to the *Late Show with David Letterman* in response to the show's call for animals who performed community service. I received an immediate response. The show's producer wanted a video of Beau showing what he could do. So I emailed a note saying, "Oh yeah, he can pull off my shoes and socks."

My mother and I videotaped Beau performing. Ever so gently he used his teeth to slowly tug on the end of my socks until they got to the end of my toes and he pulled them off. He was so careful not to bite my toes. The producer called and asked if Beau could appear on the "Stupid Pet Tricks" segment of the show in November 2003. I accepted the invitation and made plans to go.

Beau flew to New York under my seat, wearing his Texas Hearing and Service Dog vest. It is humbling to get off a plane in New York and be greeted by a limousine driver who waves a sign with your dog's name on it.

My sister from Pennsylvania met us in New York City. The show put us in a hotel across the street from Madison Square Garden, which was wonderful. We arrived at 10:30 PM with the dog, and he needed to go potty, so I asked the concierge where to find the nearest tree because we couldn't see any trees or grass. The concierge looked at my sister and me as if we were nuts. He directed us to try four blocks away from the hotel. We were Texas-born kids who didn't have a clue where we were in downtown New York.

As badly as Beau needed to go, he was too polite to pee on a car tire. Finally we circled Madison Square Garden and saw a courtyard behind a wrought iron fence on the second floor. After walking up a flight of stairs, we let Beau go off-leash to pee on a tree in this courtyard. We turned around and saw two of New

York's finest. "What are you doing?" one of the policemen asked. We introduced them to Beau and told them why we were in New York and explained our dilemma. They got a big kick out of our story. They gave a NYC police patch to me to take home to my son, who wanted to be a New York cop. We took pictures of the police officers and emailed them to my youngest child. It was just fantastic.

The next night, we walked out of the hotel room. My sister was in front. She stopped as I was going through the door, and it slammed shut, catching the end of Beau's tail. He wailed and bled. We were all freaking out. It was late at night, and my sister stayed with Beau while I went to the drugstore to find bandages. After wrapping his tail, I placed a little kid's sock over the end of it with the word "Ouch!" written on it.

Because of Beau's injury, we didn't go on *The Late Show*, but we had tickets to Radio City Music Hall to see the Christmas show with the Rockettes. The ushers didn't know how the animals on-stage would respond to having a dog in the auditorium. I explained that Beau would behave better than any child. We had third-row center seats. I had to go to the restroom during the show, and when I returned I found Beau sitting in my seat and trying to see where I had gone. The animals onstage never knew he was there.

The Letterman show producer asked us to come back in February 2004, but because of bad weather we couldn't make it. They called us again in May 2004, and Beau made his grand appearance on the show. He wowed the audience by pulling off my shoes and socks.

Our next adventure on national television came with the Animal Planet network's *Pet Star* show. We sent them a video of Beau doing service dog work. He demonstrated doing the dishes and laundry and his stock-in-trade maneuver of removing my shoes and socks. That show's producer told us right away to come to Hollywood for an appearance in December 2004.

For *Pet Star*, Beau had his own dressing room. I had gone on this trip for the fun of it and hadn't realized that the show was actually a competition with rules and regulations. We rehearsed, and afterward one of the producers said, "That's one of the smartest, most well-trained dogs I've ever seen, but you have no pizzazz." So Beau earned twenty-seven out of thirty points in the competition, and I learned that I'm not a big television star.

Patriot PAWS

In February 2005, a group of disabled veterans at the Veterans Administration hospital in Dallas were trying to train their own service dogs. They had heard about Beau, and one of them called me and asked if I could help them. The VA believed it was great for veterans with spinal cord injuries to have service dogs, so they had started a program but forgot to fund it. This was my introduction to the plight of disabled veterans in need of service dogs.

In February 2006, I founded a nonprofit organization, Patriot PAWS, to offer service dogs to veterans in need. I capitalized the word PAWS in the organization's name so it would stand out and remind people that dogs were being true patriots. At the time, my son was in the military, and my dad had been a veteran. It was after 9/11. Everybody wanted to serve our country in some way, but not everyone knew how. My way of serving came about because of my lifelong love of dogs.

I wanted to provide veterans with the self-sufficiency that comes with having a dog trained to get help in emergencies, retrieve items, open and close doors, help with chores such as laundry, pull a wheelchair, and provide something solid for a person to brace against in order to stand, walk, or sit down. I also learned that many disabled vets suffer from post-traumatic stress disorder and depression, and I knew that the companionship of service dogs could aid these vets in gaining emotional stability.

I started a small training center in Rockwall, where I could also continue my family-pet-training business. To raise enough funds to start the work of Patriot PAWS, I needed Beau to give demonstrations of what a service dog could do for veterans. We videotaped Beau, my public relations dog, and photographed his skills. Unlike a puppy in training, Beau could perform tasks perfectly on the first try. While we taped, he could correctly do the same task twenty times in a row. When the video clips played on local television, Beau's demonstrations helped to launch Patriot PAWS by inspiring people to support us.

Lori and Beau

When people see that our dogs can get a phone in an emergency and pick up a prosthetic, they become enthusiastic. One woman who had received a service dog from Patriot PAWS called and said, "I didn't have to spend the night on my bathroom floor, because my dog got the phone for me and I could make an emergency call."

All the dogs in the program have to say their prayers, pick up their leashes, and get into position to do their jobs. Sometimes, when we do clicker training and shaping behavior, we may not be communicating with a dog as well or as fast as we want. That's when I will put a dog in his crate and do the task three or four times with Beau. The dog-in-training learns by observing Beau's example. It's as if the dog is saying, "If Beau can do it, so can I!"

How Patriot PAWS Works

The first dogs we trained were rescued from animal shelters, or they were given to us. We paced ourselves when getting the word out about Patriot PAWS, because we didn't want to prompt a large number of veterans to start waiting for dogs that were not yet available. Then one day, a veteran in Colorado found our website and called us. He was desperate for help. Sgt. Clay Rankin had served for four tours in Iraq, and now that he was home, he depended on his family to help him. His doctors wanted him in a wheelchair, but he would only walk, using a cane. He refused to go out in public anymore because he might fall. His need for freedom and independence had led him to research service dogs, but the companies he found wanted thousands of dollars for trained dogs.

Clay was desperate for a dog, so we told him to come to Texas and we would see what could be done for him. Clay couldn't wait to get here.

It is important to me to have more than one dog available for placement and to be assured that any dog we place will be in a good home. The match should be perfect for both the vet and the dog. Clay really wanted a yellow Lab, and even had a photo of one as a screensaver on his computer. When we showed him pictures of the dogs we'd trained, he at first requested a yellow Lab named Luke Skywalker. Luke is soft and timid. When Clay said "Sit" in his sergeant's voice, Luke cringed and hid. Around that time Lone Star Assistance Dog Service closed, and they gave us five of their dogs. Archie, a three-and-a-half-year-old black Lab, was one of them. Unlike Luke Skywalker, Archie wasn't intimidated by Clay's commands. He wiggled and said, "I'll do it. I'll do it." During our three weeks of training with Clay, we found that he and Archie made the best team. That is how Clay and Archie became Patriot PAWS's first official veteran-dog team.

In February 2009 the American Society for the Prevention of Cruelty to Animals named Archie, at eight years of age, ASPCA Dog of the Year. The press release about this award noted, "Archie's loyalty and perseverance in helping Sgt. Rankin accomplish his daily tasks has allowed the veteran to regain his confidence and independence, move forward with his life, and continue serving the country he loves."[1] Unfortunately, Archie passed away suddenly in the summer of 2009, leaving all of us who knew him grieving over the loss of such a loyal dog.

Although we place trained service dogs with other people who have disabilities, 80 percent of our dogs go to veterans. But there was a young woman who came in a few years ago who had lost her hands just above the wrists and both of her legs below the knees. When she took a shower, she would have to ask her child to assist her. She had never had a dog. Now she gets dressed with help from Sky, her Patriot PAWS service dog. The funny thing is that she named her leg prosthetics Fred and Ginger. She tells the dog, "Get Fred and Ginger," and Sky fetches her legs and brings them to her.

Veterans from all over the United States apply for Patriot PAWS service dogs. They call us because they have seen the difference these dogs can make. Veteran contacts, such as the VA hospital that originally called for my help, recommend Patriot PAWS because they know we focus on the veterans. We make sure that our dogs have a good home and are giving service to vets because they want to and not because they're made to. We may not make as many placements or have as many dogs as the larger organizations, but we take time to work with each vet and dog as a team, so that we know the dogs we place will be happy and beneficial.

Patriot PAWS Grows

There are so many veterans on our waiting list now, and we can't do it all with only three or four volunteers. The chairman of the board of the Texas Department of Criminal Justice saw a story on dogs and prisons, and he had his agency contact many groups about the idea of letting prisoners train service dogs. They chose Patriot PAWS to partner with on this project.

Now we teach female offenders at the women's prison in Gatesville, Texas, to train dogs. Currently, twenty-two inmates are enrolled in our program to train dogs by using positive reinforcement — that is, participants learn to teach the dogs in positive ways.

The inmates acquire an occupation they can use as a new career path after their release. Our program also affects the prison guards, the wardens, and the offenders' families. The prison guards and wardens have very stressful jobs at times, and they take breaks by visiting the dorms where the dogs are housed to get puppy kisses, snuggles, and love, which eases their stress. The children of inmates can now say that their mothers are not just serving prison sentences but are also working with service dogs and aiding veterans. The father of one prisoner called me eight times in one month because he was so excited to have something positive to talk about with his daughter.

Two visiting family members cried tears of joy as they spoke to the warden after a visit with their mother. The children hadn't seen their mother for a while and had not looked forward to visiting her again in prison, because all she had spoken about in the past was "poor me" and how miserable she was in prison. After being in this program, though, she was happy and had a reason to get up in the morning. She no longer felt sorry for herself, and she could focus on helping someone. The children left the prison that day with a positive outlook.

The offenders in our program work for eighteen months training the dogs to open and close doors, retrieve bottles, and come when called. Offenders have written long letters to me explaining why their participation in this program has been an eye-opener for them. For example, an offender from the Gatesville prison wrote, "Patriot PAWS is a life link and a life-altering program! In just this past week so much has changed for me. I now have enthusiasm and a purpose. I'm not just doing my time anymore; I have a long-term goal to help people who have put their lives on the line for me. This program is amazing."

Veteran training sessions at the prison began on May 18, 2009. On that day various organizations offered to honor the veterans by providing lunch. When I tell people, "I'm going to prison tomorrow," some of them look at me as if to say, "Are you nuts?" But most of the veterans who train there are wonderful about it and get excited about this training.

The veterans spend ten days to two weeks working with their service dogs either at the Gatesville prison or at our center in Rockwall. At the prison, we have a small training center with a model efficiency apartment that contains a washer, dryer, and bed. We use the apartment for the prison trainers to teach the dogs how to perform tasks in a home-type setting. Since some of the veterans may be missing hands, we teach the dogs how to respond to both words and hand signals.

After the veterans spend two weeks at home with their dogs, I visit them there and customize the dogs to their new homes. I ask, "Why don't you let the dog open that door? The dog can open and close doors and get socks out of a dresser drawer." Or: "That dog can bring your shoes from the shower and never think he is working. He always thinks he's playing."

I teach the dogs to pick up a prosthetic. Or to chase after a tennis ball or Frisbee. Or to put toys away. I teach dogs to put dirty clothes in the laundry basket. When I orient the dogs to a service task, I use the same actions that people do when playing with them.

We are always just a phone call or email away from these veterans. We are also setting up an Internet group so that the vets can talk to each other and to me about anything that comes up, such as why a dog growled.

Every now and then, I take a picture of myself with my cell phone and send veterans a text message such as: "I'm watching you. What are you doing?" People with service dogs need to know they always have support.

I also hear comments from wives of veterans about what the dogs are doing for them and their families. The wives can actually leave the house for a couple of hours, knowing that the dogs will get the phone or provide other assistance if the vet falls.

NBC Nightly News

Patriot PAWS helped a remarkable man named Mike McHale, and our local NBC affiliate station in Dallas did a story about him. Mike had fallen out of a deer stand twenty-eight feet above a dry creek bed and severed his spine. He would never walk again. The dog we matched Mike with, Cappuccino, is a smart dog and was the first to go through the prison program.

Mike is an outgoing person and a football hero in his community. His family and friends gathered around him after the accident and held a fund-raiser to pay his initial medical and living expenses. But after a couple of years, Mike's family and friends had gone back to their own lives. When Mike went outside his home, he would notice old friends, but they'd look the other way. They knew he would never walk again and didn't know what to say to him. Public outings became painful for Mike. People didn't stare, but they avoided and ignored him. It was as if he were invisible in his wheelchair.

Mike came to Rockwall for training with Cappuccino and took the dog to the hotel where he and his wife were staying. Nobody had talked to him there for the first five days of his stay. On his first night at the hotel with Cappuccino, he went downstairs to potty the dog while his wife stayed upstairs, and six people talked to Mike. They had reason to communicate with him about what the dog could do. When Mike didn't return to his room, his wife went downstairs to check on him. Watching Mike and Cappuccino from a distance brought her to tears. This was the first time in a long time that strangers had willingly talked to Mike. She knew how much he missed being treated as a person.

The next day, Mike told this story to me. I was doing public training in Home Depot and asked Mike to do tasks with Cappuccino. We were walking down an aisle when a woman came around the corner. She asked, "Hi, how's the dog?" I noticed Mike was quiet after the woman passed us. I asked him what was going on, and he said, "She just talked to me." Instead of being an invisible guy in a wheelchair, he was now the guy with a cool dog.

When the station producers saw the Dallas segment, they told Brian Williams from *NBC Nightly News* about it. He was airing a segment called "Making a Difference" and wanted to see what we were doing at Patriot PAWS. That is how we got featured on the news program. The response to this segment was overwhelmingly positive.

Challenges and Needs

The hardest part of Patriot PAWS is letting people know I need their support financially. Fortunately people offer to donate dog food or money for it. But I can't do this work for free. It costs money to train dogs and pay for gas to make the 349-mile round-trip to the prison. The hotel accommodations and food for staff and volunteers during our prison training are also an expense that I must cover. And since so much time, energy, and passion are required for volunteers to train dogs and then have to part with them, I need money to hire more paid trainers.

It takes anywhere from eighteen months to two years to train our service dogs, and we have a long list of people who need them. I know the difference these dogs can make and wish more people wanted to give back to veterans. They gave so much to us. These young men and women sacrificed years of their lives. They stepped on bombs and lost arms and legs to keep us free to do what we want in America. A well-trained service dog helps someone for six to eight years, twenty-four hours a day. Food, play, and praise are all the dogs require in return for this valuable service to someone.

When I find a dog I think will make a good service dog, I turn him loose in a room with other dogs to see if he'll go toward a person rather than toward other dogs. I want the dog to prefer being with people. This must be a dog who wants someone to touch and pet him. Something in the dog's eyes must tell me he's willing to work.

If I can get dogs from a rescue group or animal shelter, those are my first choice. I want to give the dogs in shelters a second chance. Sometimes puppies are easier to train. I work with Lab mixes, although it's the temperament of the dog and not the breed that matters the most to me — each dog has a unique personality. But our service dogs have to be breeds easily accepted by the general public, such as golden retrievers or Labs. They have to be dogs people won't fear.

I am intuitive in selecting a dog to train. I do basic temperament testing, which takes three weeks to three months. After a while the true personality of the dog comes out. Maybe he's scared of vacuum cleaners, and I can't desensitize him. It takes time to find the right dog so I won't have to replace him after placing him with someone.

The world doesn't know what service dogs are and are not allowed to do. For example, someone came up to me and said, "You can't have that dog here in Wal-Mart." But denying entrance to a service dog is like taking a person's wheelchair away. Some people with disabilities wouldn't go out in public if they didn't have service dogs. If they drop their car keys, they have to ask total strangers for help. A dog can pick up the keys, and the person doesn't have to depend on others. I try to educate the public about these issues. When veterans or other people with disabilities leave our training facility, I give them a copy of a law book for all fifty states and ID cards with the law on the back of it. But some people just don't like dogs. Others open the door for service dogs and say, "Come on in."

Beau, Our Goodwill Ambassador

Our lives have changed so much over the years since Beau came to us. I used to have an antique bench in our bay window. Now it's filled with dog crates because I bring dogs home from prison to work with.

Things have changed for Beau too. He has grown from a scared little dog who peed on the floor in our hallway because my son's friend startled him to a dog who can walk down Broadway in New York among bumper-to-bumper people. He is the first dog my husband allowed in our house full-time, and my husband too has fallen in love with Beau.

Being a nonprofit, we are required to have board members and volunteers. Beau is our recruitment officer. Many times I walk into a store and people ask, "Where's Beau?" There will never be another dog like Beau, even if we could clone him.

At the airport, Beau is a crowd-pleaser because he has his own monogrammed luggage — a small bag he carries. He loves having kids and other people around him. He likes riding in airplanes and automobiles and runs to bring the car keys to me. At home he has a specially designed wireless pet doorbell in the shape of a paw print. Beau rings the bell to tell us he wants to go outside. When I take one of our younger dogs out for work and leave Beau at home, and I reach our truck parked between the house and garage, I hear Beau ringing the pet doorbell. He's letting me know that I forgot to take him too.

These days, Beau sleeps on his own bed in my bedroom, and he has a crate and kennel. In the past, when my youngest son would come home with friends and start making loud noises and running around, Beau would go into his crate and close the door. The rule was that, if Beau was in his crate, everyone had to leave him alone. The boys would play drums and sax, so Beau would put himself to bed.

Beau is gentle but also protective. One night after he and I did a workshop in Austin, someone tried to come into our hotel room. I had always tried to teach him to growl, but he never did. But this time, his growling woke me up. I called downstairs to tell the front desk about an intruder. Turns out that a busload of non-English-speaking tourists had checked into the hotel. One of the tourists must have thought my room was his and tried to get into it. This was the only time Beau had ever growled at anybody. He traveled with me all the time, and he knew that having someone come into our room late at night was not right.

Amazingly, Beau recognizes over two hundred words. He knows the words *forward*, *backward*, *step*, *get it*, *drop it*, *take it*, *come*, *twist*, and many other commands. I tell everybody that Beau would make the worst dog trainer look great. The education and love he's given me are wonderful. He's always reliable, performing on cue to demonstrate the tasks we train service dogs to do. Patriot PAWS wouldn't be where it is without him.

I think my passion has grown over the years as I've continued to explain what we are doing and how we work with our dogs. With Beau's help, I've gained knowledge that makes me want to be a better dog trainer and communicator. I cannot put into words the undying hunger I have for helping veterans and other people with disabilities. It makes my heart want to burst with love. Some might get excited over having a new Corvette. I get excited over a dog who wants to give service. I am happier helping others, and this makes my family and friends happier.

Patriot PAWS is about all the wonderful volunteers and the people who put a dollar in an envelope to donate after seeing me on television or elsewhere giving a demonstration with Beau. Some support us with a dollar; others may help with a thousand dollars. If someone sends a twenty-five-dollar check, it's a way for this person to give back to the community. I've learned that if you let people know there's a way to help, they will.

Daddy and I used to have conversations about making one person smile. He'd pull up to a red light and see somebody in another car. Then he would grin and wave. He did not know this person but would try to get the stranger to smile. The person might have driven away and wondered, "Who was that nut?" but he or she had smiled.

Watching Daddy putting a smile on someone's face filled my heart. While growing up with him, I got this sense of pleasure from giving. The question in our home was always: what can you do to make a difference? I was taught: Don't think about yourself. Think about others, and see if you can make one person each day smile. Give your gift anonymously. You don't have to take the credit.

These are the feelings in my heart. I believe they are in Beau's generous heart too.

MEDITATION

Because of Beau, Lori was able to fulfill her dream of helping disabled veterans live better lives. When has a dog offered you a helping paw?

My Journey with 8 State Hurricane Kate

Jenny Pavlovic, AFTON, MINNESOTA

Three weeks after Hurricane Katrina, I traveled by myself from my home in Minnesota to Gonzales, Louisiana, to help care for rescued animals. I didn't go down there to get a dog. I didn't know what was going to happen. I just had to help.

The Lamar-Dixon Expo Center in Gonzales was a series of buildings that had been rented to house rescued animals. Even three weeks after Katrina, vehicles snaked through the entrance each afternoon, arriving with more animals. I volunteered in Barn 5, an open-air building where hundreds of rescued dogs needed care.

Entering the barn overwhelmed the senses. A wave of dog smell, along with odors of sweat, urine, and feces, washed over the volunteers from countless dogs in crates set along both sides of the aisle, in the open spaces where the front walls of horse stalls had been removed. Huge fans moved the air and helped mitigate the heat. At first, the steady hum of the fans, along with the cacophony of continuous barking, made us cover our ears with our hands.

Early each morning, volunteers began feeding, watering, and walking dogs. Each dog was walked and fed twice a day, every twelve hours or so. In extreme humidity, with a heat index of 116, we fought dehydration and dizziness. There simply weren't enough volunteers to take care of all the dogs in the morning. By the end of the morning, we would have gone down one side of the aisle and started back up the other side. Usually more volunteers would show up by midmorning and help complete the second side of the aisle by early afternoon.

We would have liked to sit and comfort the dogs, but we had to keep going. There were always others waiting to have their basic needs met. However, I tried to see each dog as an individual in a sea of dogs, to look at each one and give her a comforting pat when it was her turn to go outside.

Many of the dogs had patches of hair missing, with skin discolored from chemical burns after swimming in toxic floodwaters. Some dogs were so thin that they must have been underweight before the storm and likely had been strays. Some had the scars and wounds of fighting dogs. Others appeared to be in relatively good shape and seemed to have come from loving homes. They all looked so very lost.

Late the night after my first full day of caring for dogs, my new friend Connie pulled me over to another barn aisle to help her. As I turned to go back to the aisle where I'd been working, I spotted a blue Australian cattle dog who appeared to be down for the count and running out of options. I noticed her right away because I have cattle dogs at home. She was older, a bit thick through the middle, a bit worn around the edges, but with a keen intelligence in her eyes. Her teeth were worn down, and she looked exhausted.

Connie had been the first person to sign the log sheet when the dog was brought to Lamar-Dixon, noting, "Canned food only — bad teeth." The sheet also said "9-17. 6:45, new arrival." This girl had arrived here at about the same time that I had. It didn't feel like a coincidence. Her paperwork from the Louisiana SPCA said that the dog had no identification when she was rescued from a rooftop.

The dappled blue cattle dog was burly like a teddy bear. Her expressive brown eyes drew me in. She had a red head with a white blaze, which on cattle dogs is called a Bentley. She was a mix of colors, with the outline of a black mask in front of her ears, tan points on her chest, red-speckled legs, and a beautiful white tail with blue-gray markings. She had a wear mark under the hair on one side of her neck, probably a mark left by a chain collar. Her forehead was missing a patch of hair. Her red ears were riddled with bug bites. Only a ragged edge remained where part of one ear was missing.

Was anyone looking for this girl? They hadn't found a microchip when they scanned her. Where was she from, where had she been for three weeks since Katrina, and how did she end up at Lamar-Dixon? I wondered about her all night. Somehow, I knew she was put in my path for a reason.

The next morning I checked on the cattle dog before caring for the dogs in another aisle. At first I didn't walk her or spend much time getting to know her. I was afraid to get attached and not have any lasting way of helping her. It would hurt both of us too much to give her hope and then fail. As this temporary shelter filled, animals were being exported to shelters in other states. I dreaded arriving one morning to find that she was gone. But I kept an eye on her anyway.

Soon I learned that we would have to evacuate for Hurricane Rita. Although I had flown to Louisiana by myself, the quickest way to leave was to drive home to Minnesota in my rental SUV. None of us wanted to leave, but then we learned that most of the animals too were being exported and evacuated ahead of the storm.

I didn't think the old cattle dog would survive a flight or a system of transporting animals in which she would be only one face among many. She needed someone to watch out for her, and I wanted to get her away from the coast before she could sense another storm coming. She had been left behind at least once already, and I couldn't let that happen again. After two days of clearing miles of red tape, I took her home with me to foster. Legally, she was someone else's lost property. I wanted to take care of her until her original family could be found. Once I knew she was safe,

Jenny's 8 State Hurricane Kate

I named her Kate because her red head and fortitude reminded me of Katharine Hepburn, whose biography I had recently read.

After traveling twelve hundred miles through eight states, Kate and I were exhausted when we arrived in Minnesota. I listed her on Petfinder so that her original family could find her. I took her to the veterinarian, where she tested positive for hookworms, whipworms, roundworms, and heartworms. The vet estimated that she was ten years old and diagnosed spinal arthritis and infected teeth. I didn't expect to keep Kate for long, thinking that her original family would appear when things settled down after the storms. Still, I doubted that they would have money for vet bills, and I wanted to take care of Kate's needs. New friends I'd made from an email list for Australian cattle dog lovers offered financial and emotional support to help Kate and me through some tough times.

I initially kept Kate separate from my other dogs, and I soon realized that she was not socialized to dogs. She was afraid and didn't know how to behave with them. The strong response of my dominant dog, Bandit, to her odd behavior created an additional challenge. Kate alternated between shying away from Bandit and striking at him. He responded by barking and lunging toward her in displays of dominance. I exercised the dogs separately and let them have supervised contact from a distance, hoping to gradually get them used to each other. I learned to read dog behavior much more carefully.

As I got to know Kate, I wondered more and more about her previous life. She loved to ride in my truck and felt safe there. She wasn't used to living in the house. She wanted to kill my house cat and seemed to think the cat didn't belong inside. She wasn't used to noises such as traffic, TV, sirens, or any kind of commotion. But she cocked her head and showed an interest when a rooster crowed on TV. This made me think that she must have come from a rural area, not the city of New Orleans.

As time passed and her parasites disappeared, Kate began to feel better. She learned to trust me, and we became close. Whenever Kate and I walked outside in the early morning, I was intently aware of our surroundings, scanning for anything that would upset her. Every challenge that we faced made me dig deeper inside myself. Kate awakened parts of me that I hadn't been aware of before. Caring for her was making me slow down, listen to my intuition more, be patient, and give my full attention to whatever I was doing.

In my attempts to understand and socialize Kate, I learned about Tellington TTouch methods for helping her relax and be calm, including anxiety wraps. I conditioned Kate to strange noises and situations to help her become more comfortable in her new world. I took her to obedience school. In the beginning, she was agitated to be in the same building with other dogs, but eventually she relaxed and got used to their activity on the other side of the room. I learned to be patient and protect Kate's space while she learned to be calm in new situations.

One day, Kate dug furiously in the toy box and snatched an old blue and white rubber ball. She bounced and chased it all over. This was the first time I'd seen her cut loose and play. She was feeling better, making all the trouble we'd taken worthwhile. I wondered if this was the first time she had ever played with a ball. I was overjoyed that she had the energy and the spirit for it.

I continued to search for Kate's origin but found no answers. She couldn't tell me in words where she had come from or what she had been through. I listened to my intuition and consulted an animal communicator. Kate gave the animal communicator an image of the rural area and house where she had lived. Her people left before the storm, letting Kate off her chain and leaving her in the yard to fend for herself. Her house was demolished, and she struggled in the water for a long time, ending up more than a mile from home. She didn't like to remember the terror of that time. She didn't think there was anything left to go back to.

One night, I dreamed of being tumbled about by wave after wave of water. I was disoriented and going under; I didn't know which way was up, and I felt like I was drowning. I cried out loud and woke myself. It felt so vivid and terrifying that I knew the dream had shown me actual events that had happened to Kate.

Kate was an amazing survivor and teacher. She challenged me to reach a new level of understanding dog behavior. She was affectionate yet wild. Even though she showed the courage of a survivor, she was afraid of things that I never would have anticipated, such as other dogs, traffic noises, and voices on the TV.

She took the greatest amount of enjoyment from rolling on her back in the grass, tracking a rabbit through the early morning dew, discovering snow for the first time, and chasing her ball. Kate helped me fully realize that all we really have is this present moment. She also helped me understand how important it is to socialize puppies to all kinds of situations and to other animals.

Kate did as much for me as I did for her. If not for her comforting me, I would have had a much more difficult time healing from the things I saw in Louisiana and feeling sad for the animals I couldn't help. Whenever I felt overwhelmed by the memories, I would think: at least I was able to make life better for this one dog.

MEDITATION

Don't you marvel sometimes at the resilience of dogs? What is there in 8 State Hurricane Kate's healing and ability to bounce back that gives clues for handling life's setbacks?

The Rescued Dog Who Became
My Buddha Boom!

Sage Lewis, SAINT PAUL, MINNESOTA

On Saturday, February 10, 2001, it was freezing cold outside, but I stayed inside, wrapped in a blanket and drinking a cup of hot coffee. Watching from my window as snowflakes fell, I pondered how I was going to spend my day, not knowing that my life was about to take a 180-degree turn.

The phone rang with a request for me to help rescue a twelve-week-old pup from a no-kill shelter outside of Madison, Wisconsin. The shelter director thought this puppy was a greyhound, and since Wisconsin Greyhound Pets of America had a deal with the shelter to rescue any greyhounds who came in, this puppy was deemed special. As a volunteer with that organization, I jumped at the opportunity to rescue the pup and get her into a foster home that afternoon. What I didn't realize was that this one simple choice would completely change the path of my life.

At the time, I was at a crossroads — one of many that I would experience over the next ten years. In twelve days my marriage would be legally dissolved. I felt scared and alone. Barely on my own two feet after fourteen years of sharing my life with another being, I couldn't let myself think of bringing a puppy into my home, which already included two senior greyhounds.

And then I met Maddie. I can honestly say I fell in love with her at first sight. The puppy grabbed me in a way that no other dog has ever done. Watching her exuberant spirit as she bounced around the kennel with a combination of delight and fear, I could feel in my heart how special she was. Her energy was huge, yet her body was only the size of a loaf of bread. I knew this little pup's spirit was going to enrich the life of the person she chose. Within the first fifteen minutes of meeting the energetic pup of love, I held her in my arms. Trying to help her relax, I embraced her gently against my chest. She melted into my body within moments, and I knew we were in this relationship for the long haul. There's something that happens when you've been picked by an animal. You feel it in your heart long before your brain takes over to ask, "What in the world are you doing?"

The puppy looked like a cartoon of a pit bull–greyhound mix. Her coloring was an amazing concoction called brindle, which means she looked as if she had been painted with an exotic array of tan, dark brown, and chestnut stripes on her fur. Her eyes were a deep reddish chestnut — a color I have yet to see in another dog. Later, I learned that she was not a greyhound at all but a Plott Hound — a strong, aggressive, and determined breed with a lean, well-muscled body and short, brindle coat. The breed is best known for hunting wild boars, mountain lions, and black bears. A hunting dog with a vegetarian? Sorry, girl.

Her spirit was a mirror to mine. On our first meeting, it was as if we were looking into each other's souls and recognizing someone familiar. It was amazing to witness how so much spirit could be wrapped up in such a small body. Her spirit actually filled the room.

After bringing the lively pup into my home that blustery day, I realized I hadn't experienced much love, joy, and exuberance in years. She brought with her a zest for life and a playfulness that ignited a spark in me that I'd let fizzle without realizing it.

On the second day we shared together, while this little pup

lay quietly in my lap, I glanced down at my coffee, and it hit me: she had the same rich, dark coloring as the contents of my mug, and her spirit was filled with a jolt of warmth and caffeine. In that moment, I knew Maddie was going to get a new name. Java.

Java Ignites Sparks

Within the first few moments of Java's arrival, my two senior grey-hounds, Veta and Clio, welcomed her into the pack with ease. The three of them paraded through the house and into the backyard to sniff the world together. Then Java raced circles around them until all three came back into the house and plopped down in the same bed — in unison. With two senior dogs who loved relaxing more than bouncing about and chasing things, I had forgotten how to play until Java showed up to remind me. Soon the youthful Java had me back to playing ball, playing tag, playing hide-and-seek — playing! My fears about the sharp turns my life had taken began to lessen as I immersed myself in the world of Java — loving, sharing, and exploring new places with her. What I didn't realize at the time was that she was going to help me explore the biggest place ever — my heart.

At the same time Java came into my life, I was starting to lose my fire as an elementary school art teacher and wondering what would be next for me. I had come to a tender place, after seven years of teaching, where I wanted closer connections than I could have with the five hundred students who moved through my art room each week. I also wasn't being challenged as a teacher, so I knew it was time for me to consider moving on. There's nothing worse than a teacher without fire for teaching.

Sitting in my backyard one sunny day in April, I watched Java bounce around in her five-month-old body and thought, "What can I do where I utilize both my hands and heart equally in my work?" As an elementary art teacher, I was definitely using my hands. With Java's help I came to the realization that animals were my ticket to having it all — using both my hands and heart fully. After some pondering I voiced my thoughts aloud: "I want to find a way to make money petting animals."

After expressing my wish to have a new career, I encountered the first test on my path toward its fulfillment about two months later. For months, I'd taken my dogs for exercise and group play with friends who had greyhounds. We'd all let our dogs run off-leash together on a fenced-in baseball diamond near my house. On what looked like a day of routine playtime, there were a few new dogs in the group, and for whatever reason, they chose to attack Java. Although she wasn't hurt physically, the incident scarred both of us emotionally and mentally. I felt responsible, since I hadn't been able to stop it from happening. Because of the attack, I also felt fearful about what might be next for Java and me. Java had emerged from a cloud of snarling greyhounds that day with a new spark of aggressiveness, ready to fight anyone or anything in her path.

Within the first few months after the attack, Java's lunging and growling became a big red flag signaling that I was out of my league when it came to calming her, and that we both needed help. We tried a variety of obedience classes and an aggression-reduction workshop to find a new way of working together and to help Java overcome her fears in the company of other dogs. All the while, the universe was holding as sacred my longing to work with animals. I believe that the universe plops opportunities into our laps so we can learn and grow. Java's incident with the dogs taught me how to reach out to find more knowledge, to gain more experience as a dog handler, and to take risks in going after what I wanted so that I could live a more fulfilling life. I had grown some, but a lot more was about to happen.

Getting on the Fast Track Together

Within ten months after the attack, Java and I embarked on the fast track of learning and growing. We were catapulted straight into an animal training program called Tellington TTouch — a gentle approach entailing neither fear nor force that works with animals by means of touch and movement. It helps improve mental, physical, and emotional balance and reduces fears and shifts behavior.

What I didn't know is that Java and I would both love Tellington TTouch. Within moments of our coming into our first five-day training session, the instructor had Java sporting a double-ended leash — with a clip on each end — to help guide and redirect her more easily. One end of the leash was connected to a dark brown harness, which helped rebalance her body when she lunged or pulled forward, and the other end connected to a tan head-collar to help redirect her head toward me or away from another dog. She also wore a half-body wrap, a simple elastic bandage wrapped loosely around her body in a figure-eight pattern, to give her more body awareness and comfort.

For the first time since the attack, Java and I had found a way to work together that was relaxing and safe and that produced great results. She began to focus her brain and reduce her stress levels as I learned to use specific touches on her body with various pieces of equipment, and as we practiced leading exercises, such as when I guided her through a labyrinth, around cones, and across a ladder. As a result of our training sessions, Java started reacting less to other dogs and warming up more quickly to people. I began to relax, knowing there was something that could help us.

At first, I engaged in the training thinking I was going to fix my dog. But after the first few days, I knew this work was about fixing me as well. Not that anything was broken, but Java and I both had fears that we needed to overcome. She was anxious around other dogs and certain people, in new environments, and being away from me. I was anxious about new environments, meeting new people, being judged for having a reactive dog, and

being away from Java. Leave it to an animal to help point out my fears.

For the next two years, Java and I traveled twenty-six hours in the car, three times a year, to a seven-day Tellington TTouch training. Side by side, this feisty, loyal, and diligent dog and I began to build our confidence, find balance, and discover our true selves again. Java barked less, stopped jumping up at the door, was less reactive to dogs and people, could be left out of her crate full-time, and stayed calmer when I was away from her. My heart opened more, and I could tell that the universe was preparing me for my next career. There was a resonance in my spirit each time I was in the presence of an ani-

Sage's Java

mal, and being around animals allowed me to practice my new skills. It didn't take long to discover that I had a gift for helping animals through their concerns, with love and compassion. Interacting with them was teaching me to step into fearlessness.

In a short time, my life completely changed. I quit my job as an elementary art instructor, sold my house in only forty-eight hours, and moved to Minnesota to start my animal training business. Living your life with purpose causes things to move quickly.

Years of experience working with Java had taught me to have more awareness, respect, and understanding for all beings. She had become my teacher, my Buddha. She had also acquired a number of nicknames along the way, but the one that seemed to stick the most was "Boom!" with an exclamation mark for emphasis. There were many times when Java taught me how to be a better person by being an example of unconditional love and peace, and I'd smile with joy as I called her Buddha Boom!

My bouncy, brindle sidekick reminded me daily how to play, laugh, find joy, and go after what I wanted in life — even if there were obstacles along the way. Bounding through the living room with delight, Java would glance at me sideways with a look that said "Let's play!" as she grabbed a stuffed toy and tossed it in the air. This usually happened when I was in the middle of doing something I thought was more important, like working.

My Dancing Partner

By the time Java was two and a half years old, I had started a business in the Twin Cities called Dancing Porcupine. Java eagerly helped me pick out the name by stomping her big brown paw on the porcupine medicine card during our second TTouch training session, leaving a few claw marks as a reminder. Porcupine medicine is about having faith, trusting, and letting go. Those were all the things I was learning to do with Java, as well as to be more playful. A porcupine can be docile, yet its quills remind us to be cautious. But if we're dancing, who's going to be afraid of us? Hence the birth of Dancing Porcupine. Soon clients with shy, reactive, fearful, and anxious dogs — like Java had been — were coming to me for help.

Around the same time that I began working with animals, I started to be able to hear them as if they were talking to me. My gift of telepathic animal communication grew as I continued to delve deeper within myself and learn more about who I really am — to connect more with my true essence.

While my animal practice grew, my heart expanded. My love for the world around me multiplied as love for myself magnified. My confidence shifted. I laughed and played more. I loved more. My fears decreased. At the same time, Java mirrored my growth by continuing to be more confident and relaxed in new situations and less stressed at home. Her behavior shifted from undesirable to delightful, and she exuded love more than fear.

It wasn't long after I started my business that we experienced another bump on our road. In December 2004, when Java was four years old, I had to find a new place to live within thirty days. My dream of Dancing Porcupine was really taking off, but now its success was threatened. I began to worry that I'd need a nine-to-five job in order to continue to pay my mortgage; being self-employed seemed risky.

This cloud of fear hovered long enough for me to take the time to tell the story of Java and me. I spent three solid months writing every day for hours while continuing to keep Dancing Porcupine going. By this time, Java had been with me while I'd gotten a divorce, endured a dark night of the soul, quit my job, relocated to a new state, had relationship shifts, and moved to three different homes. I had shared plenty of tears and frustrations with her. Now I wanted to share with the world our journey together. My book, *Java: The True Story of a Shelter Dog Who Rescued a Woman*, was released on February 10, 2006, six years to the day after Java first wiggled her exuberant body and spirit into my life.

While I was writing the book about Java, my finances started to dwindle, and I became afraid. I wanted more financial safety in my life, so I took a full-time job teaching art to at-risk high school students in Saint Paul, Minnesota, all the while keeping my business going on the side. I was happy for the security and enjoyed the students immensely, yet I knew in my heart that Dancing Porcupine was my purpose and passion. After two and a half years of teaching, I once again let go of my job as an art instructor and felt freer than ever.

Dancing Porcupine is now my sole source of income, and I couldn't be happier. My book is doing well and inspiring others to fulfill their dreams. In April 2009, I began hosting my own live radio show called *The Pet Playground*. Java's picture is with me at the studio every week as a reminder of how far we've come together and the impact she's had on my life. I write her advice to "breathe and have fun" at the top of my notes before each broadcast.

My business has branched out nationally and internationally. I've expanded my services to include more work with people as well as animals. I have been blessed with a beautiful array of clients and am clear that Java and I truly make a difference. I get emails from people all over the world who have read our story and thank me for the gifts that Java and I have brought them. Sometimes I get letters in the mail from kids who want to work with animals or an email from someone who just wants to know how Java's doing. Java and I have made a connection with so many, and we will continue to weave that web for years to come.

Each day, I thank Java for the impact she's had on my life and on the lives of others. Every night when we go to bed, I take some time to run my hands gently and intentionally over her warm, lean body and tell her I love her. She usually acknowledges my gratitude with one simple lick on my arm or nose as we settle into bed for the night. Then she flops her sixty-five pounds on top of my body and nudges me so I'll touch her more or looks deeply into my eyes and says, "I *know* you love me."

I don't think I could have learned the lessons I have as well without Java by my side. By being patient with me as I became more aware of and present to the moment, Java taught me to become gentler with all beings and to find that sweet place inside me where love exists and fear can be released. She has taught me to go after what I want in life. For her, it's usually a squirrel, but for me it was living my purpose.

As I write this story about our incredible journey together, my sweet girl chews on her bone next to me. I grin while thinking about what we've done together these past nine years and can feel my heart expand another notch. Her muzzle looks as if she's gotten into powdered sugar, and now my head is showing the gray hairs too. Yet our hearts and minds have become clearer, brighter, and more filled with love during the time we've shared. We've found a silent wisdom, Java and I, through our experiences together. Java is my inspiration for doing what I do in the world. She's one of the main reasons I am who I am today. To Java I say, "Not bad for a forty-dollar shelter dog, huh, girl? High five!"

MEDITATION

Dogs can be vital in helping women find and fulfill their purpose in life. Has a dog been your companion in discovering deeper meaning?

Dagnabit and Kim, a New Orleans Love Story

Kim Dudek, NEW ORLEANS, LOUISIANA

I have lived in New Orleans for thirty years. My parents met and married here, and I had always heard their romantic stories about the magic of this city. I came to attend college, fell deeply in love with the city, and never left. Following my passion for health and well-being, I opened Belladonna Day Spa in 1995. The business was, and continues to be, a success and is highly involved in community activities and fund-raising for different charities.

Belladonna gave me the freedom and financial support to begin to follow another passion of mine, which was rescuing and giving medical care to dogs. In 2004, I had four dogs of my own and began to foster dogs for various rescue groups. My gang — Burt, Ernie, Tuni, and Danny — were a good, strong, solid team who were patient and kind to the rescued dogs I brought home to heal and find new homes for. They never seemed to mind when we had an extra dog and enjoyed correcting them and teaching them the rules of the house. I always seemed to go for the very neglected, abused, and ill dogs whom others were too afraid to take on. Or I chose the huge dogs most foster families were not willing to take home — mastiffs, pit bulls, Catahoulas, and boxers.

I love to see the physical and emotional changes in dogs when they are given the proper care, food, and love. So it was no surprise when one of my employees, Billy, found Dag, a pit bull terrier, outside Belladonna and brought the dog to me. Dag wore a worn, red leather collar with his name, Dagnabit, on it and the location of his home in Florida. We decided to call him Dag.

It was obvious to me that Dag had been tortured in the usual way pit bull thugs train their dogs to fight. As a result, he was a mental powerhouse — physically and mentally intimidating, he created fear and submission in other dogs just by his presence. His ears had been scissor-cut so they wouldn't be destroyed during a fight. He had a scar around his neck but no other obvious fighting scars. He was incredibly strong and very well muscled.

Unfortunately, New Orleans has a long and not so pretty romance with dog fighting. Kept underground and not obvious to the public, dog fighting is a vicious abuse of one of the most amazing breeds of dogs. Dogfight trainers utilize treadmills and force the pit bulls and other dogs to "work out" with cement blocks and heavy chains. They hang the dogs by a wire to enrage them and make their jaws stronger.

Fighting dogs are often so emotionally damaged and physically destroyed that rescue is nearly impossible. Dogfight trainers teach the dogs to be intensely dog-aggressive and turn them into vicious balls of pent-up frustration and hatred. There are no real winners in dogfights. The dogs battle to the death or until they are beyond physical repair.

Billy called the veterinarian's office near Tampa, Florida, which was listed on Dag's collar tags. The vet's office told Billy the name of Dag's previous guardian but said that she had moved a long time ago. They had not heard from her in a while and did not know that Dag had been missing. The vet assistant gushed about how sweet and lovely Dag was and said that his ears were intact the last time they saw him. She was sorry that she could not offer any further assistance to help Billy. We searched online and waited to see if there would be any inquiries about Dag. There were none.

We surmised that Dag must have been kidnapped out of

Florida and brought to New Orleans to fight in the dark world of dog fighting. I was petrified of him. He was eighty-five pounds of solid muscle with an obvious hatred of other dogs. He would become obsessed if he saw another dog and begin howling and "pit singing" hysterically, sounding like the yodeling in a bad version of Julie Andrews's "The Lonely Goatherd" song in the *Sound of Music*, except the song never ended as long as he could see another dog. He had a mean expression of bravado on his face and aggression in his body language. This was quite a change from the picture painted by the Florida vet's report that the dog had been a calm pet when he had visited their office.

Billy took Dag to his home where he had other dogs, a blind shih tzu and a rambunctious young pug. He kept the dogs separated for months and then slowly began to introduce them after putting a muzzle on Dag. Eventually, Dag was able to be around the other dogs at Billy's house. However, he remained insanely obsessed with dogs outside his home. Billy worked the security detail at Belladonna in the evenings and would bring Dag to work with him, leaving the dog in his van parked near the door of the spa. We could hear Dag yodeling and howling whenever another dog passed the spa. Billy could do nothing to calm him during these episodes.

Hurricane Katrina

In August 2005, Hurricane Katrina headed toward New Orleans. I had rescued a shar-pei mom and her six puppies from a shelter about a week before Katrina arrived. A vet had quarantined the puppies due to the high parvovirus rate at the shelter, so we could see if the dogs were infected and needed treatment.

As Katrina approached, the vet kept telling me that he would call when I needed to take the dogs home so that we could all leave the area. He never called. I waited and waited, then I found out that he had left the city without allowing me to get my rescued mother dog and her pups.

On the Sunday night before Katrina hit, I went to the vet's office and broke the dogs out with Billy's help. I took along the vet's clinic dog, Claudia, whom he had also left caged in a bottom kennel in his office. Billy and I could not leave the city and now had fifteen dogs between the two of us. The officials had closed the highways going east beyond Slidell. To go west would mean sitting in twelve-hour traffic, since everyone was headed that way. I did not want to get stuck on the highway with fifteen dogs while a hurricane raged around me. I made the decision to stay in my house, which had been built in 1920 and still stood after being hit by numerous other hurricanes.

We holed up to wait out the storm. As Katrina approached, we all went to the second-floor hallway, away from windows and glass. We brought every pillow we could find and filled the hallway with them. And we waited. Until I heard it myself, I always thought they were kidding about how a hurricane makes the sound of a freight train as it rages. Every dog found a spot and lay quietly watching the storm. They were so calm despite the fear in their eyes. The pressure in their ears must have been incredible. They never stopped looking at Billy and me. They didn't try to hide, fight, or cry. They knew that we were in for a long, hard fight.

We got out of New Orleans on Tuesday after the levees broke, with floodwaters rising around us. My Ford Explorer carried the fifteen dogs, Billy, and me to Lake Charles, Louisiana. We were quite a sight. I had on the same clothes I'd been wearing for three days. They were bloodstained from one of my dogs cutting his paw on a broken roof tile that had landed in the yard. My shirt was also smeared with chocolate from three peanut-butter and chocolate cookies, the only food I had eaten in three days.

After we came home to New Orleans, Billy and I, his three dogs, and my five lived together for eight months in a house I owned in Marrero, Louisiana, about fifteen minutes outside New Orleans. Dag and my crew started to get used to each other. At this time, I started making frequent trips, forty-five minutes each way, to the Lamar-Dixon Expo Center, in Gonzales, Louisiana, where rescued animals were being brought to safety. The facility provided temporary shelter to cows, chickens, roosters, camels, goats, horses, ducks, turtles, rabbits, cats, and dogs. I would leave at six in the morning, when the curfew ended, and come home by seven in the evening, when curfew was back in effect.

I would return, exhausted, but all the dogs, including Dag, had to be loved and exercised because they too were traumatized from the storm. All the dogs except Dag would go out in the yard to play and run. Then Dag would run with the two brothers he was used to being around.

One day, Tuni, my female, wanted to spend time in the yard with Dag. Fearfully, I let her go with him and watched gratefully as they proceeded to play a game of chase and catch-me-if-you-can. Dag was very fast despite his bulkiness and muscle. I could see the joy in his eyes as he ran and actually played with Tuni.

But my dogs continued to be cautious with Dag. He had jerky, fast, snippy movements that I have come to know as typical pit bull behavior. These movements are often interpreted as aggression by both people and dogs, but now that I know that they are Dag's usual way of moving, I call them his "happy dance."

I began noticing signs that Dag was mellowing and becoming more trusting. At night, after I returned from Gonzales, we would sit on the sofa and watch television together. Picture an eighty-five-pound pit bull with a mouth the size of Texas and a body the size of a hippopotamus who loved to snuggle with me. Eventually Dag began to groom my dogs. He has an obsession with ears, for obvious reasons, so he would lick and clean all my dogs' ears every night. They never argued or tried to convince him that their ears were not dirty. But I was still hesitant to leave all the dogs alone without supervision. We muzzled Dag until we did not need to anymore.

Everything settled down eventually, and Billy moved back to his home with Dag. In October 2006, he called me, crying. He said that Dag was sitting cross-legged in the middle of the floor of his living room. I told him dogs don't sit cross-legged. He cried and said that he knew that and asked if I would please help him. I got a stretcher and a muzzle, and we transported Dag to my vet's.

Minutes after our arrival, the vet came out and said that we had about three minutes to get Dag into surgery. He thought that Dag had ruptured discs in his back, making it impossible for him to use his back legs. He could not be certain, because Dag needed a myelogram, which uses special dye and an x-ray to diagnose disorders of the spinal canal and cord. This test would determine if there was an injury and where the damage was. He also explained that there is a specific window of time for treating this type of condition before the dog dies or the damage is beyond surgical repair. He referred me to a neurosurgeon vet who was close by.

Off we rushed. When I looked at Dag, lying on the stretcher, muzzled, I knew that this dog and I had been through so much together and I would do whatever I needed to do to fix him. Little did I know that I would ultimately be the one who was fixed by all he would teach me.

Would Dag Recover?

After a very expensive surgery, Dag lived at the neurosurgeon's clinic for about a month and a half. I went to visit him every day, bringing cheeseburgers and words of encouragement. I watched as the light and spunk went out of his eyes. He could not walk. He was losing weight and muscle mass and would not eat. He could not control his bowel and bladder.

The vet told us to euthanize the dog, explaining that Dag would never walk again. I brought a veterinarian friend who does acupuncture to the vet's office. My friend was allowed to see Dag and do acupuncture on him.

With the first treatment, Dag was able to stand on all four legs. I cried. Dag cried. We all cried. Dag had a look of utter disbelief. His eyes were like saucers. His ears, or what was left of them, were forward and open, and he was smiling. He really did smile. As his legs at last, slowly gave out again and he collapsed to the ground, he looked up at me and licked my nose. We moved Dag out of the clinic despite the vet's continued urging that we euthanize.

Dag had always seemed to me like an invincible dog. He was strong, muscular, sharp, quick, demanding, and pushy. Now, after his injury, he was humble and small. He had lost about thirty pounds and almost all the muscle in his rear legs and butt. He had always been bright and snappy, and now he was subdued. There was no spark, no spunk, no inner fire, no self-assurance. He was broken and empty. And yet when I showed up with the burgers for him to eat, he would muster some smiles and give me a kiss to say thanks.

I don't know if it was the constant jabs from the surgeon who wanted to put Dag down because he would never walk again, or if it was my own struggle with redefining who I was and what I was doing with my life, that most affected my decision to save Dag. Katrina had refocused so much of my energy. Belladonna was rolling along, but in my heart I was still thinking about the never-ending rows of dogs at Lamar-Dixon who waited for their humans or a rescue group or just a nice person who would

adopt them. I felt I could not let Dag down. Billy was having difficulty emotionally handling the changes in Dag, and I guess I
knew in my heart that one day Dag would be mine. Katrina had
put both of us through emotional trauma. And Dag had endured
tremendous uncertainty and loss. It bonded us profoundly. I
wanted to do everything in my power to help him. I could not
bring myself to end his life without a fight. I began to put a plan
together.

The Plan

Having been a rehabilitation counselor for disabled children for
ten years after graduating from college, I knew how to bring together teams of people to improve the lives of my clients. I made
Dag my first canine client. Dag's team included an acupuncturist,
a chiropractor, a homeopath, a massage therapist, and a photographer. We called ourselves Dag's entourage.

I arranged for the vet who did acupuncture to treat Dag two
days a week with a form of acupuncture that uses electrostimulation. I called my friend who was certified in canine massage and
another vet friend who did homeopathy and chiropractic and
scheduled them to work with Dag. The canine massage therapist
came almost every day. The chiropractor wanted to give Dag more
time to heal with the other treatments, so we kept her on call until
he improved. The homeopath also wanted the acupuncturist to
work with Dag for several sessions before she started homeopathic remedies. The fight for Dag's life was becoming longer and
more arduous and expensive. At this point, Billy turned over full
responsibility for Dag to me.

As Dag continued with his recovery after surgery, he lived at
a boarding facility that was kind enough to take him in and
charged only five dollars a day. He was, however, not used to

living in a cage. We used to joke about Dag's compulsive need to control how clean or dirty he and his surroundings were. Over the weeks, I began to notice that in an attempt to regulate his elimination, Dag had stopped eating and drinking. The boarding facility did not have overnight supervision, so Dag, with his inability to control his bowels and bladder, often had accidents in his kennel. He hated being soiled but could not move himself away from where he had eliminated. This began to worry me, because he could not afford to lose any more weight, and he needed to be hydrated.

Kim's Dagnabit

At the boarding facility, the canine rehab team worked tirelessly with Dag, sometimes for four to five hours a day. We made him place his legs properly and forced him to stretch and do range-of-motion exercises. We saw very slow improvement, but the spark was not back in his eyes. Sometimes our fight to help him heal seemed cruel and unfair to Dag.

When I brought Dag home, he was still not close to being able to walk. We used all kinds of exercises, stretches, and activities, trying to give him incentive. One of our favorite exercises was to put Dag in both front-support and rear-support harnesses. Utilizing the entire boarding facility, we would make him walk with our assistance. In doing this, he had to walk past kennels filled with every kind of dog. At first I was concerned about how he might react to strange dogs, but Dag soon chose specific dogs he loved to talk to, flirt with, kiss, argue with, and smile at. The dog population changed often at the kennel, and he would have to do the evaluation process all over again. It was obvious that Dag was starting to enjoy meeting dogs. And the dogs were not afraid of him or his weird gait and inability to walk on his own.

It was wonderful to see Dag lose his old obsession with destroying other dogs. After endless months in the boarding facility and our retraining him to walk at home, he finally learned that dogs were not trying to kill him. In fact, they gave him unending support.

Another one of our exercises, which was a big hit in the boarding facility, took place in the kennel room. We would place Dag in the middle of the room with a person to support his hind legs and help him stand for as long as he could. At this point he was able to stand for five to ten minutes on his own, but his balance was not great. Dag loved to catch treats in his mouth when we threw them to him, so we started using this as a balancing exercise and a way to get him to eat. In catching the treat, he had to throw his weight to his hind legs and come up off the ground.

So there he was, in the middle of twenty kennels, with all the other dogs watching this exercise. Dag thought he was in the spotlight and would perform, catching almost every treat. The dogs started barking happy barks as if they were saying, "You go, Dag. You can do it." Ultimately we began playing the game with all the dogs. I would call their names, and they had to be ready to catch the treats. It was fascinating to watch. Dag was having fun *and* playing with other dogs.

My dogs had been afraid of Dag during those months after Hurricane Katrina, but they sensed that something was different about him when I brought him home from the boarding facility. They were patient and kind with him.

Because he'd been living in the kennel for six months, there were obvious adjustment issues for Dag at home. To help him recover, my alpha dog, who had always slept with me, gave up his sleeping spot in my bed and let Dag have it. Rocky would play tug-of-war with Dag using stuffed toys. He did not know that he was doing rehab exercises with Dag, but the effort was much appreciated. And Burt would go to Dag to have his ears cleaned, just like in the good ol' days.

Dag's Wheelchair

One day I found a wheelchair company online called Doggon Wheels, located in Bozeman, Montana. It had never occurred to me that there was such a thing as a wheelchair for dogs. The woman who owned the wheelchair company was originally from Houma, Louisiana. After hearing the story of what happened with Dag during Katrina and of his injury, she felt so much compassion for him that she donated a wheelchair.

I will never forget the day the chair arrived. Our entire rehabilitation team was there, as well as the photographer Skip Bolen, who had been documenting Dag's healing journey. We began to put the chair together. Several different companies, as I would come to find, make wheelchairs. A correct fit is imperative so that the dog is comfortable and in the right position. If a chair is not fitted properly, the dog will not make a good adjustment to his chair.

Doggon Wheels is an incredible company that works with each client until the chair is fitted properly. Its employees make chairs for every kind of injury a dog could have. They design quadriplegic chairs for dogs unable to use any of their legs, amputee chairs for dogs who have lost a limb, and paraplegic chairs for dogs like Dag, who are not able to use their hind legs. To me, these chairs are magic. They allow dogs to be independent and free, to move around, where before they were unable to move at all. They open up a whole new world for the disabled dog.

The chair is an ingenious device made of metal. It attaches to the dog with a harness, and the dog sits in a saddle made of neoprene (the stuff they make wet suits out of). The wheels act like the dog's back legs, and the dog is able to pull the chair forward using his front legs and upper body. Dogs are able to go up and down stairs, in water, in fields, and up and down curbs. There is no place a dog cannot walk in these chairs. Dag seemed to know that this device was for him. He whimpered and scooted around my living room as we wrestled with assembling it.

I will never forget Dag's first amazing day in his wheelchair and the hint of a spark that came into his eyes. With the wheelchair assisting his hind legs, he ran his fanny off from one end of my street to the other. He tore all over the church playground while we played catch-me-if-you-can with him. The nuns stood in the church windows, clapping and cheering him on. We all cried.

That day was the beginning of Dag's return to life. I retrained him to eat, drink, and potty while using the wheelchair. Then he started going everywhere — to the beach, the French Quarter, a bar, a restaurant, the park. It took a year and a half for him to master using the chair, and there were lots of bumps in the road. Being a pit bull, he at times displayed his breed's trait of horrible stubbornness and wanted to do things his way. I had to learn that his way was sometimes the best way, and that Dag needed to make decisions so as to regain confidence in his own body. His stubbornness had kept him going at times when he probably just wanted to give up.

Dag is somewhat of a celebrity in New Orleans. In 2007, he wheeled around Audubon Park during the Dog Day Afternoon fund-raiser for the Louisiana Society for the Prevention of Cruelty to Animals and won the hearts of many. The next year, we walked the 1.8 miles for the shelter's fund-raising event and raised over five thousand dollars for the LA/SPCA. I was touched by the generosity people showed after seeing Dag's courage.

Dag's Legacy

Dag has taught me much about dogs, people, and myself. He allowed us to do anything to him because he understood that we were trying to help. I have some gut-wrenching photos of him where the focus and determination in his eyes are apparent as we try to get him to relearn his gait. Dag taught me that it was okay to push him. Sometimes he did not want to do things, but with my urging he would perform. And ultimately he began to walk.

Dag has grown stronger, rebuilding his hind legs to the point that he can walk without assistance from any device. He is learning to move up and down stairs, which is very hard without full use of his back legs. For the most part, he can control all his bodily functions now and tells me when he has to go outside. We are patient and take it a day at a time. He loves long walks and forgets that these make him very tired. Then I have to carry all seventy pounds of him back home.

Dag showed me that dogs don't hold on to things like thinking "I can't" or "I don't want to." They will try as long as they know you are there for them. It brings tears to my eyes when I think of the process that was so long and difficult and of how Dag just kept going. Once he knew I was not giving up, he pushed himself, sometimes to exhaustion.

In February 2008, I opened the nonprofit charity Dag's House, where we have helped some incredible dogs develop their independence. What we do for them enables the dogs to create new lives that are different from what they had when they were healthy but still hold meaning and help them retain their spirit. I take what is given to me and, with the help of many people who have a variety of skills, work to develop and improve a dog's quality of life. If I can make a small difference in the dogs' and their human companions' lives, then I feel that I have done my job.

Every day, Dag's quirkiness makes me laugh. I like to goof around with him and know that all his previous bravado masked insecurity. It remains important to me to assure him that he is home. He had so many homes in his life, and some were unbearable. It is difficult to leave him when I have to travel, because he might feel I am not coming back. But each time when I return, Dag does his happy dance, and my heart fills with joy and gratitude.

MEDITATION

Dag recovered from a nightmarish situation with the help of Kim and many others who cared about him. How would teamwork enhance your healing or the health of others?

Euri, the Miracle Worker

Bobbi Leder, HOUSTON, TEXAS

My fourteen-year battle with chronic staph infections started shortly after I met my husband, Vern. I suspected I had picked up the bacteria from an unsanitary tanning salon, but there was no way of truly knowing how and why it occurred. It started out as dermatitis — or so the dermatologist thought, but he misdiagnosed me. As the disease progressed, it was a terrifying experience. Fortunately antibiotics cured the first infection, but this turned out to be only the start of my bacterial nightmare.

The infections kept coming, and despite my taking nearly every antibiotic available, nothing prevented them. I became a guinea pig for new medications and even traveled to the best medical centers in the United States, France, and Great Britain for further treatment, but none of the doctors I saw could figure out what was causing my chronic staph infections.

At one point, within the first few months after I moved to Houston, a simple manicure led to a cuticle infection that stayed with me for weeks. Just when I thought I was healed, I developed staph infections on my chin and ear. I went to the doctor immediately, and he informed me that, had I waited one more day, my ear cartilage would have been destroyed and my ear would have collapsed. I was glad I saw the doctor in time, but to be honest, I was at the end of my rope with the emotional and physical turmoil my body was putting me through. I had to hide from the world because of all these staph infections and their horrible effects.

Not long after my ear cartilage was attacked, my husband and I went to the annual dog show in Houston. We were avid dog lovers but knew we didn't have the time to properly care for the breed we had fallen in love with in the United Kingdom — the English cocker spaniel. We enjoyed the dog show and walked to every single booth, meeting each and every dog. We wound up staying six hours. That day, I decided I just couldn't live without a dog any longer.

We had moved twelve times in thirteen years for my husband's career, but after we moved to Houston we finally had stability and our own single-family house with a fenced-in yard. Gone were the days of living in an apartment or townhouse. After sacrificing so much because of our nomadic lifestyle, we finally decided it was time to plant roots and open our hearts and home to a dog — a dog that we had longed for all those years.

The Search Begins

I started looking online for an English cocker spaniel to adopt. I found a wonderful rescue group nearby, but unfortunately most of their dogs were American cockers, and I really didn't want to settle for a breed I wasn't in love with. I contacted the English Cocker Spaniel Club of America and filled out an application. The group's adoption coordinator interviewed me over the phone to see if my husband and I could offer a good home to a rescued dog and promised to start the search for our new dog as soon as possible. Just minutes after our phone call, I received photos and descriptions of dogs available for adoption.

My husband and I were picky; we wanted a young adult dog who was dark in color or a blue roan. The odds of finding one that fit all our requirements were slim. But my bad luck turned around that day. The adoption coordinator forwarded an email about a dog who had been put up for adoption by a breeder. In the email was a description of a cocker named Euri, along with that of another dog he lived with, but there was no photo. I didn't need a picture, though. By reading his description, I could tell Euri would be my dog.

Euri was two years old, house-trained, and a former show dog whose coat was liver colored, so I knew he would be a handsome boy. I phoned the breeder who had Euri and asked for a photo. Looking at Euri's picture on the website, I saw a gorgeous male with fur the exact same color as my hair, long ears, a long lean body, and a handsome face. I fell in love instantly and worked like mad to arrange for the dog to be shipped to me.

I had never been so excited in my life and spent the next few weeks preparing for Euri's arrival. I bought his bed, treats, food, food bowls, and anything else dog related I could think of. I was like a kid in a candy store. When the big day arrived, Euri flew in on a Continental Airlines flight. I was a nervous wreck waiting for him at the airport. When the baggage handler wheeled him out in his crate, I said, "Hi, Euri!" He panted heavily and appeared to be extremely nervous, confused, and scared.

When I took Euri out of his crate, he tried to run away, but fortunately the airport staff helped me get him into my car. He continued to pant like crazy and wouldn't even look at me. Naively, I had thought he'd be a bit happier to meet me. I petted him the entire way home and talked soothingly about anything and everything. I knew he couldn't understand what I was saying, but it was the only way I could bond with him. By the time we arrived at my house, Euri had calmed down.

When I pulled into the garage and opened the car door, Euri jumped out and ran to the house. Upon entering, he rushed in and sniffed every square inch. He was no longer anxious and seemed to understand that this was his new home. Euri hadn't tried to run away as he had at the airport. Rather, he had run into the house as if he had lived there his entire life. I immediately opened the back door so he could see the backyard. I'm pretty sure he gave the yard two paws up, because he looked happier after he marked his territory.

I wasn't sure if he would have to go out during the night, so I slept downstairs in the guest bedroom, and Euri slept on the floor beside me. Scared and lonely, he jumped up and put his two front paws on the bed every thirty minutes. Neither of us got any sleep that night, but the bond had officially been formed.

The next morning, I walked him at seven o'clock, which was unheard of for me, since I am not a morning person. Now I was full of energy and thrilled to be out with my new dog despite the early hour.

Vern was out of town on a business trip when Euri arrived, so my husband didn't meet our new dog until a week later. By that time, Euri and I had grown closer, so he was cautious around Vern at first. As they spent more time together, Euri began to trust his new daddy. Vern is the one who files Euri's nails and gives him a bath — two things he would not be able to do if Euri did not trust him.

Getting to Know Euri

Euri was born in the Czech Republic and had been purchased by two breeders in America so he could be a show dog. When he was just a puppy, he flew to America to start a new life. Unfortunately for the breeders, Euri was too big for the breed standard when he was a puppy; at one stage in his life, however, he was the perfect size and able to compete in the show world. He kept growing, though, until as an adult he was too long for the breed standard. By the time Euri was two, he had lived in three different homes —

all with breeders and a plethora of other dogs. He had never known what it was like to be an adored pooch and the only dog in the house. But when he was put up for adoption, his life changed forever.

The day after his arrival, I took Euri to PETCO to begin the pampering process and let him wander around the store. He hadn't experienced life as a pet, so walking through a pet store was new to him. Euri sniffed everything on the shelves and even tried to eat a few biscuits that were on the floor. For a spaniel, being in a pet store with all those scents must have been heavenly.

Bobbi's Euri

Euri had never even worn a collar before he flew to Houston, and he certainly didn't know any commands. But he was such a gentleman that he did whatever we wanted and never complained. I managed to teach him commands and tricks within the first two months. He continued to amaze us with his intelligence and sweet disposition. He was highly motivated by food, so teaching him to sit down, stay, come, roll over, paw, pray, weave, spin around, dance, roll over, and play dead came easily to him. Within a matter of minutes he picked up each new command because he wanted to please me — and, of course, he knew he would be rewarded with treats afterward.

Even though he took up a lot of my time because I had to brush him and clean his ears and eyes daily and walk him twice a day, I didn't mind because he had become my canine son. He followed me everywhere I went when I was inside the house. He gave me kisses and, by wrapping his paws around my neck, hugs too. Euri seemed to understand everything I said, and he acted accordingly. Once in a while I would cry as I thought about how happy he was making me and what a sad life he had had before we adopted him.

Euri overcame so many fears. I remember how scared he was that first week he arrived. Our Victorian-style house has a main living area composed of a living room, kitchen, and dining room with a front door upstairs that is accessed by climbing a full flight of stairs. When my brother-in-law and nephew came to the house to meet Euri, he must have thought they were there to take him away from me. He ran downstairs, away from the front door, and hid behind the coffee table. It took a lot of coaxing and treats to bring him back upstairs. Whenever I took Euri to a new place (for example, a dog boutique), he would jump on me as soon as we entered to let me know that he didn't want to leave my side. Today, Euri no longer hides when someone comes to the door. He is the official greeter and loves to meet new people, because he knows he has found his forever home.

Euri learned to obey our rules of not begging at the table or jumping on the couch. Somewhere along the line he managed to become comfortable with the knowledge that he is a permanent member of our family and decided it was time to get around house rules by manipulating us with his paw tricks. If we are on the couch and he knows we have no food for him, he'll give us his paw or use it to nudge our hands off our computers and request a belly rub. Whenever we have treats and he knows it, he raises his paw as a way of asking for them. He gives us a pathetic look and wags his little tail whenever he wants to break the no-jumping-on-the-couch rule. Consequently, he has become a spoiled lap dog who wraps us around his paws.

Living with Euri has inspired me to write about dogs. Each week in my online dog column, I spotlight dogs available for adoption in hopes that people will adopt their very own angel dog.

After months of being this cocker's mom, I noticed that my staph infections had not recurred. I thought it was just luck, but then several more months went by with no new outbreaks. I panicked whenever I cut myself or developed a pimple, but no staph infection ever appeared. I believed this was a miracle, and quite frankly it dumbfounded me. I couldn't understand how, in such a short time, I went from getting staph infections nonstop to having none.

Since adopting Euri in 2008, for two years I have been staph infection free, even though prior to that I battled the infection for fourteen years. Although there is no medical explanation, I believe that Euri, my guardian angel dog, was sent to heal my broken spirit and give me my life back.

MEDITATION

Have you brought a dog home who caused you to become healthier? Look at the ailments or health issues you had B.D. (before dog) and notice whether they have dissipated or disappeared.

The Blessing of a
Wheelchair-Bound Dachshund

Barbara Techel, ELKHART LAKE, WISCONSIN

The call every person with a dachshund fears, and the one that would profoundly change my life, came in the early evening, Easter Sunday 2006, when my husband John and I were fourteen hundred miles from home, vacationing at my mom's residence in Florida. My veterinarian's words brought me to my knees. "I believe Frankie has ruptured a disk in her back and needs to be rushed into surgery. She has no feeling in her back legs. Time is of the essence for her best chances of recovery."

Frankie had been staying at a kennel in our home state of Wisconsin while my husband and I were away. Yvonne, the kennel owner, had gone out to check on Frankie and noticed our dog was not moving her back end. Yvonne immediately called my sister-in-law Lori, our emergency contact. Lori rushed Frankie to my local veterinarian, who made the diagnosis.

As a puppy, Frankie was about the size of a guinea pig with short, reddish brown fur. Her fawnlike eyes were lined in jet black, which made me fall instantly in love with her. When I brought Frankie home six years ago, I knew that dachshunds could develop back problems such as ruptured or degenerated disks because of their long spines. But I was unaware of how these injuries could happen or the options for treatment.

It was hard for me to be so far from home at this time, but I knew Frankie was in good hands. Lori had rushed her to a clinic an hour away that could do emergency surgery. I found it difficult to wait for the vet's call and prayed with all my might that all would turn out fine. Nine months before, I had said good-bye to my Labrador retriever, Cassie Jo, who had died of bone cancer. The pain of that loss was still fresh. The thought of losing Frankie too was almost unbearable.

When the surgeon finally called, she told me that to determine the extent of the damage, she had done a myelogram, a procedure in which dye is injected into the spine. "Frankie has a 10 to 30 percent chance of walking again if she has surgery," she said.

I didn't think those odds were great. Thoughts and feelings began to swirl in my head and heart. Initially I believed I had no choice but to put Frankie to sleep. I collected my emotions as well as I could and said, "If Frankie doesn't walk again, what will her life be like?"

I held my breath as the surgeon said, "If she doesn't walk again, she can still lead a good-quality life with the help of a dog-cart. They are similar to wheelchairs for humans but are made for dogs."

Never having heard of or seen a dogcart, I found it hard to imagine how it would work. I told the surgeon I needed to think this through and would call her back.

I sat with my mom on the sofa and cried while trying to make the best decision for Frankie. I was fearful she might not make it through the surgery, as that is always a risk. The thought of never seeing her alive again was hard to bear. I felt sad for Frankie, wondering what the quality of her life would be if she didn't walk again. And I felt guilty about all the things I could have possibly done to prevent this, such as putting her on a better diet, keeping her off furniture, and limiting her use of stairs. I was also concerned about how to take care of a dog with special needs.

Then I became angry. "Why is this happening to me?" I cried. I had been working hard to find my purpose and had planned my life accordingly. Nine months before Frankie's back problem, I had hired a life coach because I was yearning to live a more joyful life. I had this burning question I wanted answered: "What was I brought here to do?" I also wanted to do something that might

Barbara's Frankie

make a difference in the world. Coaching helped me to discover my aspirations. Steps toward living a more purposeful life included writing a monthly column about animals for our local paper, which I loved doing. I also had been training my six-month-old Lab, Kylie, to become a therapy dog and planned to write about our experiences as a team. Kylie's calm presence made me feel more peaceful, so I thought she might be suited to therapy even though she preferred to stay close to home.

"Now I have to put everything on hold to care for Frankie," I said. "This is not fair, Mom. I don't understand why God is doing this to me."

My mom said gently, "God only gives you what you can handle." Then she added, "Maybe God meant for Frankie to be your therapy dog."

I could not picture what that meant, but something in my heart fluttered. I wondered if maybe she was right. I called the surgeon back, and Frankie went into surgery at midnight. An hour later, Frankie had made it through without any complications. The next morning, John and I were up early to make the two-day drive back home.

Caring for Frankie

I felt relieved to be reunited with Frankie three days after her injury. Her condition was daunting and scary, though, because of what lay before me in learning to care for her. Frankie's paralysis meant she had no control of her bladder and bowels. The vet showed me how to express Frankie's bladder and eliminate her stool. Frankie needed strict cage rest and many medications that were crucial for her recovery. Before I left her office, the vet handed me a brochure from a company that made dogcarts that enabled dogs to walk even though they'd lost the use of their hind legs.

As Lori drove us home, I was grateful for all she had done to help Frankie and me through this difficult time. Frankie perched on her pink pillow on my lap. To actually be with my dog again brought my heart immense joy, even though I did not know where the road ahead would take us.

I didn't immediately order a dogcart, because the vet advised me that Frankie needed eight weeks of highly restricted mobility to heal from the surgery. I searched the Internet every spare moment, trying to find the solution that would enable her to use her legs. I came across many resources that brought me some peace, such as Dodgerslist.com and HandicappedPets.com. I also discovered that physical therapy would enhance Frankie's chances of recovery, but the closest facility was more than a two-hour drive from where I lived.

I talked with my local veterinarian, sharing what I had learned. I said, "I am willing to do all I can to help Frankie. Do you know of anyone who could teach me physical therapy?" He referred me to a specialist, and Frankie and I went to see her three weeks after the surgery. She showed me various exercises Frankie could do twice a day. I also took Frankie for acupuncture. At that time, I believed helping her to walk again on her own would be the only viable solution.

If Frankie was going to regain mobility, the statistical probability was that I would see improvement in her within six to twelve weeks. Ten weeks into doing all I could, nothing had changed in her back legs. It hit me hard that most likely I'd be caring for a special needs dog for the duration of her life. I found this difficult to face and started to feel sorry for myself. I knew it would be tough taking care of a dog who needed help going to the bathroom. The idea of adjusting my schedule to help her overwhelmed me. My husband and I would never go on a vacation, because no one else could take care of Frankie. Besides, what if something happened again while we were gone? The thought was too frightening.

After ten weeks of trying all kinds of therapy, I was taking Frankie through her exercise routine when it suddenly occurred to me that she had never once felt sorry for herself. Instead, she had remained the same sweet, happy dog and had adjusted beautifully. In that moment I knew I was being sent a sign from God. I had a choice. I could feel sorry for her and me, which would not change the situation, or I could look for the blessing in why this tragedy had happened to us.

Two weeks after my epiphany, I ordered a dogcart for Frankie. I chose one from Eddie's Wheels. Their carts are custom-fit, and the story of how they began their company touched my heart. The back part of the dogcart has a padded seat with two openings that Frankie's hind legs slide through; two small wheels jut out the back. A cloth strap snaps across the front of her chest, and two aluminum bars, one on either side of her body, support her. A padded bar arches across her upper back to connect the two side bars, which are held in place by two aluminum pins. The dogcart turned out to be the answer to my prayers. After Frankie was hooked up to it, it took only five minutes of enticing her with treats before she was running on her front legs, using the wheels as substitutes for her nonfunctioning back legs. Frankie was free to be a dog again and do just about everything she had done before her injury. My heart filled with happiness to see her enjoying life to the fullest again.

At first, I was apprehensive about taking Frankie out in public. I didn't know how people would react to a dog in a wheelchair. I thought they might think it mean or strange. I also wondered if they might say, "Poor dog," and feel sorry for her. I didn't want that. I knew Frankie was happy. She looked a little different now with the dogcart, but using this device had not changed her personality or spirit. I had also begun to realize that Frankie's dogcart might offer an opportunity to show others that animals with disabilities deserve a chance.

One morning about a week after Frankie learned to use her dogcart, I held my head high and took her to our local farmers' market. I was pleasantly surprised. People expressed compassion for Frankie, and many wanted to know her story. Even more amazing was how children responded. They were curious and loved the fact that Frankie could walk with wheels.

After hearing why Frankie's spine stuck out, because of muscle atrophy, one young boy said, "Well, it doesn't matter what you look like on the outside, but what is inside." This wise comment struck a chord deep inside my heart.

Finding My Purpose

I had wanted to write a nonfiction book about the journey with my first dog, Cassie Jo, and the lessons she had taught me. But now I understood that Frankie could have a big impact on children and help them overcome their own challenges. Even though

I had never written a children's book and was scared to attempt it, my heart told me that this was the direction I was meant to take. I knew that if I didn't follow through I would regret it at the end of my life.

I wrote a children's book about Frankie to encourage children to use her positive example to overcome their own challenges. I believed she could also help children understand people with disabilities and learn the meaning of compassion and kindness. I designed a program centered on the book's messages and started visiting area schools with Frankie, which I continue to do to this day. Frankie helps kids know they can always make a positive choice no matter what obstacles life hands them.

The rewards are beyond anything I could ever have imagined. Frankie and my other dogs have taught me that life is abundant in beauty and love. Frankie has given me confidence I never had before. Despite the loss of her natural mobility, not once did her spirit diminish. Frankie persevered despite her challenges, and I realized she didn't worry about what others thought about her. I had been shy for most of my life, often worrying about other people's perceptions of me, but as I watched Frankie be the same dog she had always been, despite her new way of walking, it gave me the confidence to stand tall.

Life has a way of coming full circle. One day I remembered my mom's words of wisdom: "Maybe God meant for Frankie to be your therapy dog." After continually witnessing firsthand how gentle and calm Frankie is around children, I decided to expand her mission and mine.

In September 2008 Frankie became registered with Therapy Dogs Inc. We continue to visit schools, but now I also bring her, as a therapy dog, to hospitals and hospice patients and the elderly. She has opened my heart even wider to what this thing called life is all about — living your truth, reaching out to those in need, and living in the moment of each precious day. It makes me smile to think that I learned all this from a wheelchair-bound dachshund.

MEDITATION

Frankie and Barbara's journey inspires us with its simple truth — physical disability or illness doesn't have to diminish a person's or a dog's spirit. What have you observed when dogs are forced to handle adversity?

Better with Barney

Linda Panczner, TOLEDO, OHIO

That which doesn't kill us makes us stronger. Live long enough, and this saying will most likely test you. Hopefully, you will have some kind of support while trudging through those challenging times. Mine was Barney, the devoted, goofy, kindhearted dog God lent me during my trying transitions.

Barney and I — I still like the sound of that — were a devoted couple for twelve years. I know that sounds silly to people who don't associate with dogs, but those who do will understand. Before and after Barney, life was and is a present I've been grateful to receive, but Barney gift-wrapped it in festive layers of celebration.

We came together when the puppy I would name Barney showed up at the nursing home where I worked. Wednesdays were pet therapy days, and each week a volunteer from the humane society brought a dog or cat to visit. My office was in the administrative wing, but I made a point of going to the residents' area every Wednesday to meet the animal of the week. It wasn't only the residents who benefited from the caresses of the animals who welcomed our attention and gave back to us.

Each week, I argued with myself whether I should adopt the animal who offered entertainment and comfort. I always let pragmatism prevent me from bringing one home. Thinking about the cost, the time commitment, the fact that I lived alone (which meant this burden would be entirely on me), the number of years

I'd have to invest in providing for a pet, and other logical considerations held me back. Meeting Barney changed all that.

The day Barney was brought to the nursing home, I couldn't say no to him. He was an eight-week-old, pudgy, squirming bundle of black fur, pink tongue, and wagging tail that alternately nuzzled and yipped while sitting in the lap of each resident. I waited impatiently for my chance to cradle the wiggling fur ball, and then I didn't want to hand him back. This Great Dane–Lab mix reached me on a deep level, and I knew he was the dog for me. Despite the well-rehearsed objections that had kept me from weakening in the past, I was drawn to the pup by something stronger than reasoning. It wasn't just infatuation; there was a purpose and connection that defied explanation. I gave myself permission to do something wacky and wonderful, and yes, emotional. Forget logic, wisdom, and caution: I had to share my life with this dog. We were meant to team up; it was as simple as that.

Not so fast, though — Barney was going back to the humane society, where the rule for adopting any pet was first come, first served. I arranged to leave work early that day and drove directly to the animal shelter. Sure enough, another family in the market for a dog was looking at the possibilities, and one of the children claimed my intended puppy. Fortunately, she was outvoted by the rest of her family, who chose another dog instead of the puppy who had called to me. After I filled out a lot of paperwork and wrote a check, Barney became my official roommate, and we left for the ride home.

Tucking Barney into an improvised nest fashioned from a box and a towel stored in my trunk, I secured the box to the floor of the front seat so I could look down on him as I cautiously drove away. I felt giddy, guilty, and giggly. "That's my dog down there," I thought, and then: "What have I done?" I had no regrets, but plenty of apprehensions. Could I train him? How would he handle the first night? What about his first day alone when I went to work? These and other questions played in my mind, but out loud I spoke nonsense words to my new puppy. I sang the song "(How Much Is) That Doggie in the Window?" and other silly tunes until we reached home.

Though my hasty acquisition of Barney began with an emotional rush, I had been researching the issues of dog ownership for some time. However, I had not purchased any supplies. So after Barney fell asleep in a box I had fashioned into a temporary bed within a partitioned area of my kitchen, I drove to the nearest store that stocked pet supplies. I racked up a hefty charge on my credit card for the basics and then some. It's hard not to be swayed by the unnecessary yet adorable merchandise designed for puppies, and I was a sucker for much of it. Laden with bagfuls of dog paraphernalia, I hurried home to introduce them to my new charge.

Barney's First Season

I discovered that the usual bleak months of winter brightened considerably with a puppy in the house. Instead of dwelling on a job that frustrated me (except for the Wednesday pet visits), and a personal relationship that seemed to be detouring from the intended altar, I was focused on Barney as a source of delight. His play was as fascinating as his quieter times, when he curled into himself, or me, for a snooze.

I exhausted the word *cute* when describing Barney to everyone and contrived excuses for bringing him along with me wherever possible. Surely the entire population would be as mesmerized as I was by this magnificent dog, so I wanted to make sure everyone enjoyed an opportunity to meet him. Turns out, I was wrong about that. Some people just don't like dogs. Go figure.

One day, a man opened the door to a convenience store while I stood outside with my gangly four-month-old pup. Barney showed his affection for this stranger by jumping up and planting his muddy paws on the man's chest. The stranger was not destined to be Barney's (or my) friend. I forget the man's exact words, but they were colorful. Seeing his shirt, now turned brown with streaks of mud, my face turned red. Only Barney remained unconcerned with the mischief he had caused. I concluded that it was time for puppy obedience classes, which would educate me as well as my dog.

Linda's Barney

Over time, the Great Dane portion of Barney's genes was expressed in his height and size. Too often, he'd clear the coffee table with one swipe of his long tail. Then, pleased with himself, he'd look at me comically with one ear pointing straight up and the other bent forward.

As Barney grew, so did the unpleasant complications in my life. The job fizzled around the same time that a relationship ended and a close relative and I had a parting of the ways. With the downturn in my personal life complicated by a dismal economy, I had to make some changes, which included a move across three states. Thanks to family members who arrived to help me load my belongings into a caravan of three vehicles, I accomplished the twelve-hour trip in one day. But what a day.

My car wasn't ideal for a dog as big as Barney, even when empty. Once I'd crammed it with my possessions, there wasn't much room for driver and dog. For most of the trip, Barney, who sat in the backseat, preferred to rest his head on my shoulder. This may sound sweet but wasn't so enjoyable after several hours on a hot, muggy summer day in a car without air-conditioning.

The first few months at my new locale were bumpy. I had to take a series of temporary placements until a secure job materialized. I rented a house until I could complete the harried process of purchasing one, and I also coped with a series of family misfortunes. Barney didn't have to do anything special to lighten the load I carried; he just had to be there, and he sure was. The devotion he showed me, the exuberant greetings he bestowed on me whenever I returned home: these acts of dedication cushioned me and lightened my burdens.

In the ensuing years, there were other rough patches, including the stress of another meaningless job, another move, and what was for me the ultimate trial to endure — the death of my father. Barney became both my pillow and snuggle blanket throughout, absorbing my tears and pain.

Barney the Wonderdog

By the end of our first year together, my gentle giant of a dog had grown to his full height and size and proven to be as smart as he was talented. In obedience classes he might be puzzled by the day's new command, but by the following week he would outshine the other dogs in demonstrating it. During the week in between classes, we'd practice the skill in the backyard until he perfected it. When our daily work was over, the Frisbee, hula hoop, or tennis ball would come out, and we'd play catch-and-throw.

Anyone observing us would have concluded that I was crazy about this dog. He became my best friend, and I enjoyed hanging out with him. We went on walks every day. He loved car rides too, so on weekends I drove us to parks and open areas, where I sought places tucked away from the public so he could run free. Whether he was cramming his big frame into a kiddie pool so he could lap at the water, or galloping through a creek, the Labrador retriever portion of his genes had supplied him with a love for water. Another of Barney's joys was to roll from side to side on his back, his legs splayed in the air, while emitting pleasurable groans in his loud bass voice.

At the end of the day, he didn't care if my full-size bed was not adequate for a person and a dog of his size who took up excessive space when he sprawled out on it. However, we compromised, and I let him lie at the end of the bed. In his last year of life, he inched his way up alongside me on occasion, and I admit that I allowed it.

Wonderdog that he was, not every undertaking was successful. I tried to teach Barney to run alongside me as I biked. I certainly couldn't let him run full out on the leash, because my two short legs couldn't keep up with his four long ones. I figured that, by biking, I could keep up with my speedy dog, and both of us would enjoy a workout. That was the plan. After Barney jumped with excitement on the front of my bike, and I flipped forward onto the pavement, I gave up that idea.

Barney also failed in the independence category. He and I lived alone, so he was used to being alongside me when I was home. Whenever I walked beyond the reach of his leash, his vocal objections could be heard for quite a distance. One summer I brought Barney on what was supposed to be a four-day campout with my family. Any time I tied his leash to a tree or handed it to a relative so I could walk the short distance to the bathroom, he cried so loudly that I had to take him with me into the stall. We left the campsite after one night.

The same thing happened when my neighbors held a garage

sale and I offered to help. With Barney closed up in my fenced yard, I sat with my neighbors across the street in their garage, out of his sight. Somehow he climbed the tall metal fence, crossed the street, and loped up the neighbors' driveway amid the startled customers. My neighbors and I laughed at the typical Barney behavior, but some of the shoppers stepped back when they saw a big, loose dog approaching. I could have told them, "Don't worry, he wouldn't hurt a fly." Actually, he ate flies, but he loved people.

Barney Keeps Me Going

Barney made me feel special during both the fun episodes and the times when I struggled to fit in. I had become a person with baggage, but Barney shouldered the weight with me. Compared to my happy-go-lucky "kid," I was weighed down while experiencing some of the hard realities that inevitably show up in life. Sometimes, several challenging situations slam into a person at once, as if to test how well we can endure the trying times. As I juggled the loss of my father, another unsatisfying job, a health concern, and middle-age realizations that there *are* limitations after all, Barney kept my teeter-tottering life balanced with his compassion. He softened the hard corners and lightened my darkest moods.

Whether we were playing, working, or enduring, we shared the process of becoming better. The goofy dog who was always ready to walk or play matured into a wise companion who enjoyed more subdued moments, such as when he curled up beside me on the couch with his head on my lap and sighed in contentment. I too found relief as I learned that, after coping with major problems, I had become more capable of understanding and forgiveness. Eventually my journey of discovery led to new options that seemed custom-fit for me. I looked forward to settling into a phase of satisfaction with my best friend, who would benefit as well. But it wasn't meant to be.

How does a woman write about her pet's demise without a flood of tears and a box of tissues? I can't, which is also why I sometimes skip over the death scenes in animal stories. So I won't go there, except to mention that Barney died at home in familiar surroundings, and I was with him.

Toward the end, I had to leave his side to take a bathroom break. Afterward, I sank to the floor in the living room, with my back against the sofa, for a quiet sob. I planned to return to Barney, who was two rooms away. Instead, Barney, on wobbly legs that barely held him up, stumbled into the room and made his way to me. He swayed until I helped him lie next to me with his head in my lap. After all the times I had leaned on him when I was stumbling, now he sought my support. Despite the weakness and pain he endured on that last awkward walk, he managed to make it through one room and then another and collapsed by my side. Barney let me know I was still his number one priority. That last noble gesture, the final tribute Barney paid, consoles me along with a multitude of memories.

As I look back on that period of my life when I transitioned through various changes, it is not the tumult I remember but the companionship of my dog. The mind has a way of buffering the bad times and highlighting good times. I am blessed with scrumptiously wonderful recollections of my time with Barney.

MEDITATION

Sometimes, it's not the heroic acts that we remember the most, although we're grateful for them. Instead, it's the dogs and people who quietly, consistently, go the distance with us. What dogs have made your life better?

For Two Dollars She Was Mine

Debra J. White, TEMPE, ARIZONA

For a scabby mutt called Maxine, I paid two dollars to a woman hawking vials of crack cocaine. That was September 19, 1988, when I worked as a social worker in a South Bronx neighborhood pulverized by poverty, illicit drugs, and more gang members than police could arrest. Already living on a shoestring budget and nearly crushed by student loans, I had planned to take Maxine to the city animal shelter. I lived in a one-room apartment and struggled to pay rent and utilities. How could I afford a dog? By the time I got home, the skinny dog with a sparse brown and gold coat, who appeared to be a sheltie mix, had melted my heart. I kept her.

A veterinarian pronounced Maxine to be young and in good health, so I introduced her to my jogging routine to channel her boundless energy. Maxine adjusted to my morning schedule in Central Park, but as a vagabond she had absolutely no behavior training. She chewed nearly everything I owned, including shoes, toothpaste tubes, jackets, a Rubik's cube, and books. When I opened the front door of my apartment and clutter greeted me, those sparkling eyes and wagging tail always won me over. How could I be mad at her when she kissed my cheek?

At night, Maxine snored, making rousing, loud noises. I often wondered what she dreamt about. And no matter how many comfy dog beds I bought her and put in the bedroom, she would sleep only in the bathroom. I would move her bed closer to mine, where I thought she'd be more relaxed, but each time she'd resist and return to the bathroom. I finally gave up and put her bed in there, because she seemed happiest near the bathtub.

Maxine wolfed down each bowl of kibble as if it were her last. As a stray, she had scavenged food from garbage cans and any other place where scraps might be available. Undoubtedly, she had spent many days being hungry. I promised her that, as long as she lived with me, she'd never have to worry about her next meal. Still, she didn't seem to understand, and I felt bad watching her inhale food even though life was good for her now.

Blessed Maxine

Every October, the Cathedral Church of Saint John the Divine in New York commemorates the feast of Saint Francis of Assisi, the patron saint of animals, with an elaborate blessing ceremony. Members of the public and their pets are invited. I figured Maxine needed all the help she could get, so a few weeks after adopting her we walked to the massive church on West 114th Street and Amsterdam Avenue from our West 87th Street apartment. The cathedral was packed with people and pets, and we slid into a pew filled with dogs. All the barking and yapping rattled those of the feline persuasion, although a few brave cats sat on their owners' laps or in carriers, looking as if they were not quite sure what to make of the barking bedlam.

I adored her, but Maxine was a handful. Expecting her to sit quietly was asking too much. She wanted to play with her canine companions, who seemed eager to engage in a hearty game of tag. After I coaxed her into some semblance of order, we waited for the service to begin. Every time the choir sang, so did Maxine. Tipping her head back, she howled like she knew all the words. People would have laughed out loud, but it was church, so they smiled instead.

Singing with the choir didn't calm her down. About halfway through the service, Maxine spotted a fluffy white dog sitting a few rows behind us and was determined to play with him. Catching me off guard, Maxine jumped over the pew, sailed through the air, and landed next to her new friend. The two dogs licked each other and seemed ready to romp and roll. I got up and retrieved Maxine, who wailed as if she were leaving her best friend. Church was never this much fun when I was a kid. I finally left before the service was over, because Maxine caused such a ruckus. I waited outside for a pastor to bless her. And he did.

Friendly Maxine

In spite of her being an apartment destroyer, Maxine saw everyone as a friend, someone to love. Better yet, she just wanted everyone to love her. She couldn't get enough affection. Weeks or months of street life had deprived her of human companionship, and on our daily walks she greeted our neighbors as if they were her best friends.

When Maxine and I lived in Boston for a while, I found out that the Massachusetts Society for the Prevention of Cruelty to Animals, the shelter where I volunteered, had a pet therapy program. Because of her friendliness, I considered enrolling Maxine in the program. She passed the initial introduction, and we became an official pet therapy team.

As a therapy dog, Maxine cheered nursing home residents with her spunky personality. One elderly woman saved treats for Maxine's weekly visits, including apple pie and bacon slices, every bite of which my dog enjoyed. Maxine trotted through each resident's room and brought smiles to patients whose lives had been shattered by illness, injury, or advancing age.

At an animal shelter fund-raiser, Maxine and I won an award

in the owner/dog look-alike category. An avid jogger, I wore my jogging outfit and dressed Maxine in running shorts, T-shirt, and sneakers and draped a bandanna around her neck. We were quite the team, even if she refused to keep the sneakers on her feet.

Maxine the Healer

Maxine and I shared a special bond. Rescued dogs generally show unusual loyalty to the people who save them, and Maxine was no different. She followed me all around the house, often sitting outside the bathroom while I showered. As I left for work, she'd throw herself at the door and whine.

During the years when we lived in New York, we jogged together in Central Park. Sometimes we drove to the country to buy fresh apples. I had her picture taken with Santa as part of a fundraiser to benefit an animal shelter. In the winter I bought Maxine a doggie sweater so she'd be warm. On paydays I always treated her to a box of snacks. I loved that dog.

On January 6, 1994, after Maxine and I had moved to upstate New York, we were taking our usual stroll after work when a car struck me and threw me into a ditch. I was rendered unconscious. Maxine was unharmed but shaken. Neighbors said she refused to leave my side and she licked the blood oozing from my head. After the ambulance came and collected me, she whimpered and whined as it sped off. Fortunately, friends cared for her throughout my two-month absence.

During my hospitalization, friends persuaded the doctors to allow Maxine to visit. Although I have no memory of her bedside calls, friends said I knew her name. At the time, I didn't know my own.

When I came home nearly two months later, I was on the verge of slipping into a deep depression. How could I, an active, vibrant thirty-nine-year-old woman live as a person with disabilities? I had jogged nearly every day and had run the New York City marathon three times. I'd biked up mountains in Colorado. And now I could barely walk. I had always earned my own living, often juggling two jobs at once. I had once held an important corporate position. After I'd switched careers to social work, I tracked down pregnant crack addicts in dangerous neighborhoods to help them receive prenatal care. I'd intervened in domestic violence cases. I had had excellent recall and rarely kept an appointment book. Now, I couldn't tell one day from the next and wondered what would become of me.

Debra's Maxine

But Maxine's warm nose nudging me to get out of bed made the difference. Slowly, I let go of my anger and realized my life had a purpose. Maxine needed me, even if no one else did. Someone had to feed her, and I was that someone. Walking her was no longer an option, so I sat on the front steps while she took care of business. Slowly, I got off the pity pot because I realized that patients I'd seen at the rehab center were injured much worse than I. At least I'd been able to come home, while some of them had not. I could have easily died that night when I was struck, but hadn't. My old life would never come back, and I'd have to create a new one. Maxine would be there to help me.

There was a period of time when I moved around a lot.

Whenever I relocated, Maxine always came with me. Leaving her behind was never an option. She enjoyed hamburgers minus the pickles at fast-food restaurants during rest breaks on our trips to a new location. No motel ever refused to rent me a room because of Maxine. And yes, she slept in the bathroom at the Holiday Inn.

Riding through Life with Maxine

In the years that followed my accident, Maxine took my disability in stride. We went everywhere together. She rode on my three-wheeled motorized scooter in a little space on the floorboard, in front of my legs, where she could squeeze in her twenty-five-pound body. She sat there looking like the happiest dog in the world. As she aged, my scooter became as vital for her outdoor activity as it was for mine, since walking was no longer easy for her.

After Maxine and I settled in Tempe, where I live now, she became sick. First, it was thyroid disease. Then diabetes hobbled her. Twice-daily shots of insulin prolonged her life, but kidney and liver failure soon followed. Maxine lost her struggle in February 2001. I cried for days. How could I live without my beloved Maxine?

Other unwanted dogs have needed me since. I've loved each and every one, but Maxine will always remain in a tender place in my heart. That was the best two dollars I ever spent.

MEDITATION

Many of us spend a lot more than two dollars on our dogs. What are the many reasons why your dog is worth it and a bargain at any price?

The World's Best Talking Dog

Jill Allphin, CORVALLIS, OREGON

Yes, dogs talk. I never knew that until my dog, Jerome, told me.

Dad's hunting dog, Tiki, never talked, at least not to me. But when I was eight, she had pups, and Dad gave me first pick of the litter. They were all sleek and black like Tiki, except for one — Jerome. He was curly and brown like the collie down the street but had a black face. That's how I got the world's best dog.

For a few days he slept and squeaked and gulped milk like a wiggly pig, but the minute his eyes opened, he started talking. I'd been rubbing my cheek against his soft fur, and when I held him out to look into his shiny little eyes, he told me he loved me and how happy he was to be my puppy. Then he put his paw on my face.

I was so surprised that I took him in the house to tell Mom and Dad. They laughed, and Dad hugged me and chucked me under the chin. Then he gave me a wink, which surprised me even more and made me wonder if Tiki had been yakking away to him all along.

Mom told me to take Jerome back outside. I couldn't believe it. I knew Tiki never came indoors, but Jerome was just a puppy. Surely her no-dogs-in-the-house rule didn't apply to him. But it did. And there was no use arguing.

I loved my mom and she loved me, but sometimes she could be so mean. She thought dirt was next door to the devil, and that dogs did nothing but lie around on the ground all day sucking up dust like powder puffs sucked up face powder. It wasn't fair. I stomped outside, planning to stay really mad. But Jerome started crying and told me I was making him sad, so I said, "Sorry," and petted him, instead.

Over the next two years, Jerome grew from a bouncy fuzz ball into a big, strong dog of seventy-five pounds. He had thick golden brown fur, a broad chest, a plumed tail, and the most beautiful brown eyes. His black face made him look thoughtful and serious, which he was. He was smart too and taught me lots of things.

For instance, he taught me that *all* dogs talk. That's why God gave them mouths to tell us when they're scared, hurt, excited, or mad. And tails to tell us how happy they are to see us. And ears to tell us they're listening to every word. And eyes to tell us they understand how we feel and that they always feel the same way we do. And paws to put on our knee so that we pay attention to them, or to scratch the door with so they can go outside — for those dogs who are lucky enough to live inside.

After Jerome told me about the others, all dogs started talking to me. But Jerome was still my best friend. He was fun and serious and followed me everywhere. We played, we hiked, we swam, we biked. We lay on the big sandstone barbeque under the chinaberry trees and read every horse and dog book in the school library. We sat in the irrigation ditch when it was dry and dreamed about getting our horse ranch and planned how exciting our lives would be. And whatever my problems, Jerome always knew just what to say to make me feel better. But somehow we couldn't get past Mom's no-dogs-in-the-house rule.

We tried everything. Jerome was as nice as pie to her, always doing whatever she told him and wagging his tail too. He never licked her legs like Tiki sometimes did, which made her jump and yelp as if she'd been bitten. I pointed out a million times what a good dog Jerome was. I even tried to get Dad on my side, since he actually liked animals. And I waited to ask him in front of Mom, so he'd tell her it was okay. "Dad, can't Jerome come in? Dolly gets to come in." (Dolly was my cat.)

"Dogs don't belong in the house," Mom would say before Dad could answer. "That's why they have doghouses."

"But you don't like to let Dolly indoors, either. And there's no such thing as cathouses."

Dad busted out laughing. Mom gave him a look that shut him up, and he ducked into the kitchen and started laughing even louder.

"Dolly comes in sometimes," she said.

"But she can't stay in. You won't let her sleep with me."

"Well, cats are..." She paused. I knew she was going to say "dusty" or "dirty" or something. "Nocturnal," she finished.

Dad came back into the room, grinning.

"No cats in bed!" she said and went out.

"Dad, it's not fair! Jerome never gets to come in. Mom always wants everything so clean." I spit the word *clean* out of my mouth like it was an old, buggy mulberry.

"Aww, honey," Dad said, "she worries about you. Dust isn't good for your asthma." He patted my head and left to look for Mom.

We had moved to California when I was four because my dad had found a good job there. I had my first asthma attack in the middle of the night. I remember sitting on my mom's lap as my dad drove fast down dark streets with no other traffic. I remember the hospital with its bright lights and people rushing all around. I remember getting a shot.

After we'd moved back to Arizona and become poor, there were no more hospitals. Although having asthma was no fun, it became just another part of life. I'd take cough medicine and sit up in bed for three days and nights, sucking in air and coughing.

Rocking back and forth helped somehow. So did sipping gallons of water. So did Dolly, who sometimes jumped in my bedroom window and sat with me while Mom was out of the room. Dolly always calmed me down and made me forget about my breathing problems, but she was a scaredy-cat. Whenever she heard Mom coming, she hopped out the window quicker than a jackrabbit, so Mom never saw her with me. Jerome bravely continued to whine outside, telling me he wished *he* could come in.

Whenever I became sick, Mom would do almost anything to make me feel better. She'd bring out the old Halloween noise-maker with the jack-o'-lanterns painted on it, so I could call her without using the air in my lungs. And she'd come right away whenever I rattled the noisemaker. She'd bring me books and magazines, fix my favorite foods, and buy grape Popsicles for me from the ice cream man. Mom would read Dr. Seuss books to me, which I still loved even though they didn't have any horses in them. But she wouldn't change her no-dogs-in-the-house rule. Instead, she'd sit on the side of my bed, wipe my face with a cool washcloth, and explain how dogs with all their dust, hair, and dander could make me sicker. She'd promise that I could play with Jerome as soon as I got better.

But one summer day when I was ten, Jerome changed everything. I was stuck in bed, trying to breathe and desperately wishing I could fall asleep, when I heard a loud grunt. I looked up to see Jerome sailing through my bedroom window. He landed on my stomach, folding me up like a lawn chair.

He stuck his wet nose on my cheek. I flopped back into my pillows to get away, but he was as big as I was. I shoved him off my chest into the bed beside me and concentrated on sucking in enough air to stay alive. He inched forward, trying to lick my face and hands. It was gross and funny. I started to smile and tried to fend off his kisses with my arms and hands. I was surprised, because he had never been much of a licker. From between my elbows I could see his worried eyes and his face frowning fiercely. His tongue licked everywhere on me at once. My laughter burst out like a bad lawn mower trying to start. I grabbed him in a headlock. "No," I whispered, between gasps. "Lie down. Quiet."

Eventually Jerome settled in beside me with his chin resting on my stomach and my hand stroking his head. His eyes were peaceful, and so was I. My breathing slowed. I had drifted off to sleep, when Mom's scream ripped through the room. Jerome jumped to his feet and hopped all over the bed and me.

"Bad dog!" Mom screeched. She bounded toward us with her arms flailing. "Get down!"

Jerome bolted off the bed and ricocheted around the room with my mom right behind, shrieking, "Out! Out!" They ran from the room, and I heard the front door open and slam shut.

Mom staggered back into my bedroom. Her hand grasped the front of her blouse over her heart. "Are you all right?" she asked. "How did that dog get in here?"

As if to answer her question, Jerome soared through my window once again and knocked me flat. Mom screamed and leaped back, catching the door frame to keep from falling down. I was the first to recover. I sat up, grabbed Jerome around the neck, and wrestled him off of me. We struggled while I reestablished my headlock around his neck. Only then did I realize that my mother had been screaming the whole time.

Then Mom's shoes came unglued from the floor. She flew at us as if she intended to yank Jerome away with her bare hands and drag him out the door. Like she would ever touch a dog! Sure enough, she stopped short of the bed. "Jill, let him go. You can't breathe all that dust."

I couldn't talk just then because I'd used up most of my air in the wrestling match with Jerome, so I made my meanest face and stared her down.

"Jill, let him go. You're hurting him!"

Mom's eyes were wild. Jerome's eyes were bulging. I slipped my arms down around his shoulders, and he could breathe again. The two of us stared at Mom for a minute.

Finally Jerome started talking. He told Mom with his eyes that he loved me more than anyone in the world and had to come in to stay with me because I was so sick. If she threw him out, he was just going to keep jumping back in. And that's how it was.

Then I told Mom with my eyes that I didn't care if he was dusty, because Jerome's dust never bothered me a bit. And I felt much better already, because I had such a good dog. And she just had to let him stay inside with me until I could go out and play with him again.

Then Mom told us with her eyes that letting a dusty dog in bed with a kid who is having an asthma attack could not possibly be a good idea. It made no sense and wasn't smart, but she could see how much it meant to us.

Then she kept blabbing away with her eyes, not knowing we both understood her thoughts perfectly. She said she could tell it wouldn't be easy to keep Jerome away from me, because it was way too hot to close the window. In fact, she was sure that if she tried to throw him out, it would only make things much worse before they could begin to get better, if they *did* get better. And crazier things have been known to happen. "Okay," she said at last with her mouth. "Jerome can stay, but if you start coughing..."

Jerome looked at me. I told him with my eyes that I would drink a whole swimming pool full of water if I had to before I'd ever cough in front of my mom again. He smiled at me, big and wide, with his tongue hanging out, and told me how happy he was. I smiled back, and we hugged tighter. As Mom turned to leave the room, I looked over Jerome's shoulder and saw that she was smiling too.

That was the last time Jerome ever jumped in the window. After that, Mom always opened the door for him.

MEDITATION

When have dogs spoken to you in ways that you could definitely hear? How have they eased your pain even though no one else could?

THREE

Embracing Life

You shaggy Loveliness,
What call was it? — What dream beyond a guess,
Lured you, gray ages back,
From that lone bivouac
Of the wild pack? —
Was it your need or ours? The calling trail
Of Faith that should not fail?
Of hope dim understood? —
That you should follow our poor humanhood,
Only because you would!

— JOSEPHINE PRESTON PEABODY, "To a Dog"

Judy and McDuff:
Soul Mates on a Spiritual Mission

Judy McFadden, HENDERSON, NEVADA

Adam and Eve, Romeo and Juliet, Bogie and Bacall, Judy and McDuff. Judy and McDuff? What do famous soul mates have in common with my Scottish terrier therapy dog, McDuff, and me?

In his book *Soul Mates: Honoring the Mysteries of Love and Relationship,* Thomas Moore describes a soul mate as "someone to whom we feel profoundly connected, as though the communication and communing that take place between us were not the product of intentional efforts, but rather a divine grace. This kind of relationship is so important to the soul that many have said there is nothing more precious in life."[1]

Soul mates are usually thought of as lovers, family members, or close friends. The possibility that they could have fur coats and four legs never entered my mind until I met McDuff. Characteristic of soul mates is the willingness to provide comfort, support, respect, companionship, and unconditional love. I believe soul mates also share common goals and should bring out the best in each other. I see no reason why this description can't apply to relationships with our animal friends. When I think about my life with McDuff, I see that an animal can have the qualities of a soul mate. A soul mate should make you a better person, and that is what my extraordinary and mystical Scottish terrier therapy dog did for me.

I've never experienced with any other pet a unique and close relationship like the one I had with McDuff. From him I learned valuable, life-changing lessons about unconditional love, unselfish service, and the value of looking beyond appearances. During my nine-year journey with him, we experienced a powerful physical, emotional, and spiritual connection. A connection that wasn't broken even after his death.

The Best Christmas Gift Ever

On Christmas Day 1994, all eyes focused on a tiny black ball of fluff as he scampered across the floor. The only danger to him at the time was the oversized Scotch plaid bow around his neck that kept tripping him. One week later, I would be holding his life in the palms of my hands.

When the rambunctious McDuff was nine weeks old, a tiny dog biscuit lodged in his windpipe and cut off his air supply. I saved his life by applying the Heimlich maneuver. Holding him around his tiny body, I began pushing in with my thumbs just below his rib cage. After about three compressions, I heard a dull thud as the biscuit dislodged. McDuff became deathly still. His small chest quivered, raised, and fell as he began to breathe again. Over the years, McDuff repaid me time and again for saving his life.

As a good soul mate would, McDuff offered comfort to me throughout my acrimonious divorce. He eased my stress after a man broke into my mother's home one cold February night and she ran screaming into the darkness to a neighbor's home. She collapsed while waiting for the police to arrive and was rushed to the hospital, where she spent the next twenty-seven days in ICU. McDuff consoled me during Mother's lengthy hospitalization after the home invasion, a medically induced coma, and the agonizing decision to disconnect her life support after consulting with, and at the advice of, her doctors. A precedent-setting jury trial followed, and the man's conviction on a charge of involuntary manslaughter was the first of its kind in Clark County, Ohio.

Throughout all these experiences McDuff provided his special brand of therapy and support. On stubby legs he ran to meet me, wagging his tail like crazy, his eyes celebrating and welcoming my return. Holding and petting him calmed me down after long and stressful days at the hospital's intensive care unit or the staid courtroom. His furry back against my leg soothed me as we slept in my bed.

Mystical McDuff

McDuff was a spirit dog. As a soul mate, he had mystical gifts, and this quality revealed itself the day I first picked him up. As I held the puppy at eye level, he faced me and his eyes burned into mine like two smoldering embers. I thought, "I wonder what adventures we two are going to have together." But this thought hadn't come from me. It had come from McDuff. I hastily put him down and never told anyone about the strange incident. At the time I didn't have a clue about the extraordinary creature in my hands and the road we would travel together.

Native Americans believe there are spirit animals, or totems, who have special powers to join with an individual and act as a guide in the physical and spiritual world. I feel close to Indian culture because my maternal great-great-grandmother was a Chippewa. When I was an adult living in Ohio, I often attended powwows.

At one powwow an Indian woman who had long, shining black braids and wore a beautiful buckskin dress and beaded moccasins stared at me for a while. Then she smiled and exclaimed, "You belong to the Wolf Clan." Dogs are descendants of wolves, and I've felt a love for and attraction to both all my life. Perhaps my being a member of the Wolf Clan is the reason McDuff chose me to accompany him on his mission to bring comfort and joy to children, the elderly, the sick, the disabled, and the dying.

I grew up a coal miner's daughter in southwestern Pennsylvania. I always knew where the wild things hid and pointed them out to my unsuspecting playmates. With my dogs I roamed the woods and rolling hills around Beeson Works, a row of weather-beaten, wooden company houses outside the small town of Uniontown, Pennsylvania. I assisted my cats when they gave birth, rescued baby birds when they fell from the nest, and tamed and rode the half-wild horses who hauled loaded wagons out of the coal mines.

McDuff and I Find Our Destiny

Because I grew up seeing neighbor help neighbor in my coal mining community, which was home to people from diverse nationalities and cultures, it's natural for me to want to serve others. I found a unique way to combine my love of animals and helping others by becoming a volunteer with Therapy Dogs International.

I knew without doubt that McDuff would make a fantastic therapy dog and believed that he and I were destined to bring comfort and joy to others. He differed from the typical Scottie in many ways. He was the Will Rogers of canines when it came to aggressiveness: he never met a dog he didn't like, and he adored cats. I've seen a little child walk up to him, bend over, and pull his protruding eyebrows without his moving a muscle.

After moving to Henderson, Nevada, outside of Las Vegas, in 2000, I started our therapy dog visits. I would walk with McDuff into nursing-home rooms that seemed to be shrouded by dark clouds. The residents in them were like wilted flowers, and they rejuvenated under the refreshing rainfall of McDuff's unconditional love. Many were alone in the world with no one to visit or care about them. I listened as they told me about the pets they had been forced to leave behind. Or the dogs they remembered from childhood decades ago. All the while tears would stream down their cheeks as they caressed and hugged McDuff. Being able to embrace a creature who gave unconditional love and wet, sloppy kisses lifted their spirits and warmed their hearts.

I watched as patients in hospitals, their faces distorted by pain and numbed by fear, lit up and smiled at the sight of McDuff. They reached out weak hands to pet him, forgetting their health problems for a little while. I knew they missed their pets at home and longed for the day they would be reunited with them.

As I approached a room at the end of a hospital corridor one afternoon, a nurse stopped me and said, "The old man in that room refuses to respond to anyone. Maybe you'll want to skip him." I turned to leave, but McDuff had other ideas. He pulled on his leash and led me into the dimly lit room.

"Hello," I said. "Do you want a visit from a therapy dog?" No response.

I looked past the rumpled empty bed. A frail, white-haired man slumped in a chair near it, almost invisible under the white blanket draped over his shoulders. As I turned to leave, McDuff dragged me across the room. He put his head on the man's knee and wagged his tail like crazy. Without moving his head, the man stared at the black, happy creature standing in front of him. That was all the invitation McDuff needed.

"McDuff's a therapy dog and visits patients in the hospital," I said, thinking this explanation might get a reply from the man.

He ignored me, but his eyes never left McDuff's steady gaze. Slowly he raised an emaciated hand and placed it on McDuff's head. The two of them stayed that way for a while, ignoring me completely. The room remained quiet but somehow seemed brighter. I waited a while for the man to speak. When he stayed silent, I said, "Have a good day."

McDuff and I turned and walked away. After we reached the door, I heard a feeble voice say softly, "Thank you." Tears sprang to my eyes at the thought that I had considered not visiting his room. The nurse and I hadn't known that the lonely, withdrawn man needed a therapy dog visit. But McDuff had.

McDuff's Miraculous Visit

McDuff not only connected with the elderly and sick but also bonded with those thought to be beyond reach. His ability to love unconditionally was demonstrated by his amazing connection to individuals in Project PRIDE (People's Right to Independence, Dignity, and Equality). This nationally recognized program offers relief from the stress of round-the-clock medical and personal care to the parents of young adults who have severe mental and physical disabilities due to illnesses or accidents.

Project PRIDE is operated by Opportunity Village, the largest private, nonprofit community rehabilitation program in Las Vegas. On our first visit to Opportunity Village, I opened the door by the Project PRIDE sign and entered a room with McDuff trotting at my side. My heart beat faster as I looked around the room. I wanted to bolt out the door. I was thinking: "What have you gotten yourself into? Don't panic. Be calm and hang around for a little while. Then you can get out of here. You can't just turn around and leave now."

Before my eyes were five young adults, the only ones in Project PRIDE at that time. The number of clients has grown since then. The young adults had been described in an article in the *Las*

Vegas Review-Journal as having the most severe mental and physical disabilities in Nevada. Although they were in their early twenties, the young men and women looked like children. Most of
them could not walk, talk, use their hands, or see. They were in-
continent. Some were fed by tubes.

McDuff looked past their appearances. He pulled on his leash
and guided me around the room. I followed him over to a young
man strapped to a tilt table and started a conversation with the
woman feeding him. "His name is Chris," she said. "He can't walk,

talk, see, or use his arms.
He wears diapers." Since
Chris was so far off the
floor, I picked McDuff up
to bring him closer. Not
knowing what to expect,
I watched McDuff's un-
wavering stare at Chris —
that same strange stare he
had given me when I first
looked into his eyes.

After several minutes,
McDuff bent over and be-
gan tenderly licking Chris's

Judy's McDuff

face. Something unusual about the licking struck me right away.
It wasn't the typical way I'd seen him lick others. Softly, deliber-
ately, and in a much slower and more focused way, he stroked
Chris's cheek with his tongue. That's when something unexpected
happened that shocked us all.

"Come here, quick! Chris is smiling!" the woman shouted out
to her colleagues, almost dropping the jar of baby food she had
been feeding him. The staff rushed to us, their eyes wide in
astonishment as they watched Chris and McDuff in their own

private world. They told me that Chris had never before reacted to anything by smiling.

Perhaps the way McDuff licked Chris's cheek with his soft, warm tongue conveyed an entirely different sensation, one that Chris had never before experienced. Or maybe it was something else — McDuff's acceptance and unconditional love coming through. I realized that although I hadn't known what to do here or how to react, McDuff had. I knew then that we would return to Project PRIDE so he could provide more comfort and joy in his own special way.

Only one of the clients in the Project PRIDE program was unable to respond to McDuff that day. The others reacted to him by smiling, pulling his ears and long eyebrows, attempting an as-sisted throw of a ball for McDuff to retrieve, or just basking in the enjoyment of being stimulated by him. The young adults' amazing response to McDuff resulted in a television news feature on Las Vegas's Channel 3 and front-page coverage in Henderson's *Anthem View* newspaper. The switchboard at the facility's head-quarters jammed the day the feature aired on television. People called to learn more about McDuff and how they could volun-teer with their dogs in the therapy dog program.

On our subsequent walks in the park, at visits to the vet, or anywhere I took him, someone would come up to me and say, "Is his name McDuff?" I was used to him commanding attention. Scotties have a presence unlike that of any other dog — the way they walk, those superlong, erect ears, the flowing beard, and pro-truding eyebrows. On many earlier occasions, adults or children had stopped and pointed to McDuff and told me that they had an image of a Scottie on a sweater, pajamas, or other article of cloth-ing. But now, McDuff was becoming a celebrity in his own right. And he loved every minute of it. He dashed up to each new ad-mirer to receive attention.

McDuff Takes Me on His Next Adventure

It broke my heart to leave Project PRIDE, but I began a job at the Clark County Courthouse in Las Vegas. I knew working a full-time job would conflict with the program's hours and make it impossible to go to Opportunity Village with McDuff. We concentrated on doing therapy dog visits to nursing homes and assisted living facilities in the evenings and on weekends.

K-9 Therapists of Las Vegas informed me of a new program called Reading with Rover, where dogs listen to children read in an effort to encourage them and improve their skills. Kids who were uncomfortable reading aloud in front of others in the classroom, or who were otherwise struggling with reading, entered the program upon nomination by their parents, teachers, or caregivers. The bond that developed between the students and the dogs made it fun for the children to read to the dogs, who didn't judge, tease, or criticize. Since the program took place on Saturday mornings, participating with McDuff fit into my work schedule. And McDuff loved children. In fact, he loved everybody and everything — except birds, monkeys, and the UPS truck.

Steven, a chubby fifth grader with reading difficulties that had caused his self-esteem to plummet, met McDuff in the Reading with Rover program at the Paseo Verde Library in Henderson, Nevada. Every Saturday morning, McDuff sat and listened with those long, erect Scottie ears while Steven read to him for forty-five minutes. Some of the kids said their dogs were silly, stepped on their books, tried to lick them while they read, fell asleep, or didn't listen. Not McDuff. He was all business while listening to Steven. The Reading with Rover coordinator remarked after observing him in the Reading Room: "McDuff's more serious than the other dogs. He seems to know this is important."

After reading to McDuff every Saturday morning for twelve weeks, Steven went from a D average to the honor roll. When their sessions together ended, their bond remained unbroken. Every other weekend, Steven's mother picked up McDuff on Saturday morning for a sleepover at their home, where my dog was treated like royalty.

Saying Good-Bye to McDuff

I lost my soul mate, teacher, and companion on Halloween morning 2003. I released him after I found that he had a recurrence on his foot of the skin cancer for which he'd been treated six months earlier. He'd had a partial foot amputation then, and I decided not to put him through the leg amputation the veterinarian had recommended. There was no assurance that the cancer had not spread. As much as I dreaded it, when the medications failed to control his pain, I knew I had to make the decision about his life.

Fortunately McDuff made that decision for me early one morning by means of the uncanny telepathy we shared. I awakened in the wee hours one morning and heard McDuff on the floor by the foot of my bed. For years, he had slept on the bed with me, but he had stopped that custom after the surgery. I think the weight of his body put too much pressure on his healing foot when he jumped down to the floor.

Slipping from under the covers and onto the floor, I went down on my hands and knees in front of him. At his eye level, I looked at him waiting for me to speak. "Duff, this isn't working," I said. "Things don't look so good. The pain pills aren't helping even though I've doubled the dosage. It's killing me to see you suffer like this. I think it's time."

He licked his foot, raised his head, and gazed deeply into my eyes. We stayed locked together that way for a while. Then he lowered his head, and his tongue caressed the back of my hand one time. Looking up, he stared deeply into my eyes again — the last time I saw that wise and mystical stare. The communication I received from him in that moment was: It's all right with me. Do what you have to do.

I called the vet's office the next day. Anyone who has traveled this heartbreaking road knows how unbelievably fast the euthanasia shot works. In a snap of the fingers, my beloved soul mate was gone. When I walked out of the vet's office, I left McDuff's body behind, but I carried his spirit in my heart.

McDuff's Spirit Lives On

On the sad day that McDuff died, I thought our connection had ended, but he stayed on the job. He came back to jerk me out of the debilitating grief and despair I felt over losing him. One day, in the early morning hours, as I cried softly I heard him bark twice. I felt the weight of his body as he walked along the side of my bed. The familiar head thrust under my hand, something McDuff had always done when he wanted me to pet him. Then, in the blink of an eye, he was gone. A feeling of ecstasy surged through my body and replaced the grief and heartache.

It's said that the bond between therapy dogs and their human companions goes deep. All I know is that McDuff crossed the bridge between life and death to bring comfort and snap me out of my downward spiral. I found consolation in knowing that he had been in my bedroom. After this experience I still cried for him at times, but it was different. I knew McDuff wanted me to stop feeling sorry for myself and get on with my life. And that's what I did.

Other eerie events occurred after McDuff's death. A magnificent rainbow-colored arrangement of flowers was delivered to my home with a card that read, "Thinking of you. I know how much you are loved. McDuff." I couldn't believe my eyes and read it again.

I called the florist and asked about the card that had come

with these flowers. She said she would check on the wording and get back to me. The woman called after several minutes and said, "The card should have read, 'Thinking of you. I know how much you loved McDuff. Linda Peck.' I'm so sorry. This has never happened before." The woman at the flower shop had no way of knowing about the spirit dog whose name was on the card. She didn't know that he had reached out to me through the one thing that never failed to lift my spirits — flowers.

Another incident reminded me that, even after he was physically gone, McDuff continued to bring love into people's lives. Darlene, my petite, silver-haired neighbor, had fallen in love with McDuff as she watched us on our morning walks. Shortly after McDuff passed away, Darlene was diagnosed with lung cancer and she moved to Oregon to be near her family. Two years later, I received a Christmas card from her. It did not contain tidings of great joy. Darlene wrote that her lung cancer was terminal and she didn't have long to live. Then I read something in her letter that sent chills up and down my spine. "I keep McDuff's picture in front of me. As my tears fall, I just know he is in my arms comforting me. Maybe I will see him soon."

McDuff and I traveled together on his mission that affected the lives of so many. Judy and McDuff. Soul mates in life and in death. My heart broke when I lost him, but the life lessons he taught will always be with me.

MEDITATION

McDuff continued to offer comfort to Judy even after death. Have you seen a vision, felt a presence, or had a dream which showed you that your soul mate lives on?

Lady, the Miracle Dog

Virginia Consiglio, FAIR HAVEN, MICHIGAN

In spring 2004, I met a couple of real estate clients and our relationship blossomed into friendship, partly as a result of our common love for the boxer breed of dog. Months after closing on a home, they opened Wigglebuttz Boxer Rescue. My lakefront home is along Anchor Bay in Fair Haven, Michigan, which neighbors the New Baltimore area. Our homes were only a few miles apart, which made it convenient for me to become an official foster volunteer for the organization.

One day, Lady, an abused, fawn-colored, female boxer with floppy ears who was nearly a year old, arrived at the rescue center. A nervous, scared dog, she had been found abandoned, chained to a tree, and starved. Her ribs protruded vividly through her thin coat. Mine was the only place available to provide the care she needed, so I took her home with me.

Within twenty-four hours, Lady had chewed through my leather sofa, destroyed my favorite pair of heels, and proved that she was not housebroken. Each time she did something unacceptable, I would sit on the floor and talk to her, all the while petting her and assuring her that I wasn't upset. I wanted Lady to be certain that my home was a place of peace before I tried to train her. It was obvious that she had never received the love she deserved and had not been taught right from wrong.

When Lady finally allowed herself to relax, she became eager to learn and easy to train. All she needed was for someone to have faith in her. After we began our work together, she never destroyed or even chewed another item that wasn't edible.

Shortly after she caught on to the house rules, Lady began to show me that she was grateful for her new home and for me. When I went to bed, she would watch my every move. She'd come to my side of the bed and place her front paws at the edge of the mattress, wanting me to put my hand on her head. She'd seem to melt in the warmth of my touch, and I would feel her body weakening. Then she would lay her head down by her paws in a position that made her look as if she were praying. I came to believe that this gesture was how she gave thanks.

I didn't realize how much I had become attached to Lady until someone showed an interest in adopting her. My heart dropped. She was so peaceful and happy. The last thing I wanted was to betray her trust in me. I had to keep her. The rescue organization allowed me to adopt her, and Lady became my little girl and sole companion to my male boxer, Cash.

Our Spiritual Journey Begins

On May 28, 2009, Lady, Cash, and I began an amazing spiritual journey that changed our lives, and I experienced a miracle. At that time, I strongly believed that, when I put my worries into God's hands, I could trust him to respond. One day, however, when I suddenly realized that Lady had gotten out of my backyard, my faith and trust in God were put to a test.

I ran down the street frantically looking for her and discovered that she had wandered across the highway. I turned my face away, hoping she wouldn't recognize me and run toward me, recrossing the highway in the process and possibly being hit. That was when I heard screeching tires. Horrified, I watched a car slam into her beautiful little body. She flew into the air and landed on her back as she hit the paved road. After tumbling a few car lengths, her body continued to slide uncontrollably down the road.

As I rushed toward her, she startled me by jumping up and running away. Confused and frightened by the honking horns, Lady continued to run past our house. I could not keep up with her. She jumped over anything in her way until I lost sight of her. I searched for hours, worried that she was surely injured, but found no sign of her anywhere.

Lady must have been terrified. She no doubt thought she had done something wrong and probably feared being beaten as she had been before her rescue. All I wanted was to hold her in my arms and tell her everything would be okay. Because I was too anguished to go home without her, I continued to search throughout the night, going back home periodically to see if she had returned on her own. The following day and for weeks after that, I drove up and down each street within a five-to-seven-mile radius, looking for Lady. I searched two or three times a day for at least two hours each time.

My daughter Theresa, son-in-law Greg, and their three boxers drove from Chicago to help with the search. Theresa and Greg had been active members of our local boxer rescue group before relocating to Chicago. My grandchildren, Matthew, age seven, and Madison, age fourteen, came in from Georgia that same weekend to visit me for six weeks. We spent much of our family time trying to find Lady. They were as determined to locate her as I was, since they had two rescued boxers as family members. I prayed that God would watch over Lady and bring her safely back home.

While I looked for Lady on the road, my youngest son, Michael, called all the vets in my area. He informed them that Lady had a microchip implanted by Wigglebuttz Boxer Rescue and left information about how to contact us. He also contacted animal shelters, humane societies, and sheriff's departments in

Saint Clair and Macomb counties, informing them of Lady's situation. He explained to everyone that the dog was injured and asked people to please look out for her. He continued to follow up every other day for an update of their findings.

Two foster moms of rescued boxers went to the shelters to make sure there were no mistakes in the shelters' identification of boxers, so that neither Lady nor other boxers would be left there, mistaken for other breeds. Volunteers from Wigglebuttz and Mid Michigan Boxer Rescue also helped by posting a description and photos of Lady on the Internet and notifying other animal rescue groups. Each day, the volunteers encouraged me with their phone calls. So many people, including my neighbors, did all they could to inform the public about my lost boxer.

I placed Lady's cage and favorite rug in front of the house near the sidewalk, hoping she could catch their scent and sniff her way home. It was difficult to stay focused on my work, knowing that Lady might be injured, cold, frightened, and hungry. I needed to know she was okay.

Thumper Shall Show the Way

The fields near my home are swamps and heavily infested with mosquitoes. It was nearly impossible to search this terrain on foot. When more than five days had passed since her disappearance, I knew that time was growing short if Lady had sustained injuries. I created a flyer with her photo on it that asked those who saw the dog to contact me. My grandchildren and I placed a flyer at every business within a ten-mile radius and hand-delivered about eight hundred to homes. If anyone had her, there was no excuse not to contact me. If someone had found and intended to keep Lady, I hoped the person's neighbors would do the right thing and call me.

I received phone calls almost daily and was happy to learn from many of them that Lady had been sighted, she was alive, and her legs seemed to be okay. Unfortunately, she would always be gone from where she had been spotted before I could find her.

A man who called said he saw Lady in his yard. A woman said Lady had been sitting on her deck, looking into the house through a patio door. When the woman had approached her, Lady had run off. The woman described her home, and I was relieved to learn that it resembled mine — a little white house on the lake. Lady must have remembered the lake and used it as a landmark, which indicated that her memory was functioning well.

One call came from a person who had seen a fawn female dog drinking from a ditch. I drove to the area where the dog had been spotted, shut off my headlights, and waited a while. When I didn't see Lady, I drove into a church parking lot the next street over and parked. That was when I noticed a Michigan state trooper had followed me. I turned on the interior lights before the policeman approached my window, so he could see that I had Cash with me. I didn't want the officer to be startled if Cash growled or barked.

After I had Cash settled so he wouldn't jump, I opened the window and talked with the officer. I explained that I was searching for my dog, who could possibly be hurt. After listening to my story, he asked for identification. I grabbed one of my business cards, which was attached to a house-shaped magnet; it was the only thing that had my phone number on it. I told him to call me on my cell phone if he saw Lady. He seemed genuinely concerned about the dog. But then he asked again for identification, and this time he clearly added, "Such as a driver's license." That's when I realized I had given this trooper my business card instead of my driver's license. He laughed with me as I apologized, and he said he understood.

Because I remained determined to find Lady almost a month after her accident, people began to feel sorry for me. I continued to search for her as if it had been only yesterday when she jumped the backyard fence. Was I supposed to get a grip and move on? I kept praying, asking God to lead me to her. She was trying to come home but had lost her way. Lady was somewhere, depending on me to rescue her again. The phone calls from those who read my flyer and responded to it were instrumental in my long-term search. They were my compasses. They kept me posted about her possible location, and as long as the phone calls continued, I had evidence that Lady was still alive. The calls renewed my determination to keep looking for her.

Virginia's Cash (left) and Lady

On the twenty-seventh day after her disappearance, a man called to say he had seen Lady in his yard the night before. After thanking him I drove down his street. A private, thirty-acre parcel of land was at the end of the street. Later that day, a dear friend and I came back and trespassed on the private parcel — a field of tall weeds with a narrow path. Slowly and cautiously, I drove into the field.

Out of nowhere, a cute little bunny, whom I mentally named Thumper, jumped in front of my truck and stopped. He stared at me for a second and then began to guide me as I drove behind him along the trail. Fearlessly he hopped in front of my car, stopping and looking back constantly to make sure I followed. My friend startled me by laughing at the bunny's behavior. I hadn't seen her lately, and she had no idea of the turmoil I had been going through during the past weeks.

I told her that God was sending his animals to help me locate Lady. This awesome little bunny remained only feet ahead of my truck. The trail eventually led to an area with a dried-up creek bed. The bunny scampered off into the weeds, so I turned back. I could have walked the trail and followed him, but the mosquitoes there were unbearable.

Later that evening, I wondered about the significance of my bunny guide. Since people had tried, and failed, to lead me to Lady, following the bunny made me feel that I had been placed on a different spiritual level — one where God's creatures could help me. My children and grandchildren must have thought I had lost touch with reality, because now my imagination came alive with the thought that Thumper had shown me the way. I searched the Internet for an aerial view of the property to see where the trail the bunny had taken would lead and discovered that the path ended at a cemetery. I decided to go back the next morning.

Before I went to sleep that night, I reflected on the day. I didn't know what God wanted of me. "What is it I need to see? What am I supposed to do?" I thought, "What part am I not getting?" That night, I got down on my knees to pray — praying on my knees was something I hadn't done in years. I needed spiritual discernment, knowledge, and guidance. After nearly a month of searching, I gave myself one more day to find Lady. I knew I couldn't do anything more than I had already done.

The Last Chance

On day 28 after losing Lady, I woke up feeling hopeful. I started out early and drove directly to the cemetery. When I arrived, I got out of the truck and walked around, calling Lady's name and wait-ing for her to come running to me. Rain began to fall, accompa-nied by thunder and lightning. I returned to the truck and started covering my usual route, driving up and down streets and look-ing for Lady. Although I felt frustrated at the lack of success, I still searched, thinking that I might catch her seeking shelter. I knew she hated getting her feet wet and was terrified of loud noises. But she was nowhere to be found.

As I drove back home, I cried out, "God, what do I have to do to bring Lady back home? Do I need to forgive myself?" Wow, where did that come from? Was I blaming myself? I began to cry, feeling terrible. I should have paid more attention to what was going on around me. The day she got out, the backyard gate had been secured. My patio is elevated, which led me to think Lady must have braced her hind legs against the edge of the patio and leaped over the fence, which was about five feet away. My regrets included wondering whether, if I had caught her in the act, I could have protected her from the harm she'd endured once she got out. Our beloved animals, like our children, depend on us to keep them safe. I freely gave my sadness and guilt over to God. In that moment, I forgave myself and with great relief released all to him with an understanding that this act of surrender must be one of the lessons I was supposed to learn.

Less than an hour later, a woman called to say that she had just seen Lady running down her street. I took Cash and drove to the cemetery. This was not where the woman had sighted Lady, but I felt drawn to look there again. Standing near the back of the cemetery, I yelled and clapped. Cash barks only at strangers and other dogs, and never on command, so I was not expecting any-thing from him. While I called for Lady, Cash stared at me. He waited until I had yelled her name and clapped my hands a few times. Then he shocked me by barking twice. A few more times,

I clapped and he barked, as if we had made a pact to help each other.

I couldn't see anything, but because Cash was behaving out of character, I sensed that something was happening. A rustling sound came from the field. Moving bushes attracted Cash's attention. He began to pull me in the direction of the sound. I held him back; I was afraid a coyote might be concealed in the bushes. I did not want Cash to be attacked, so I decided to head back toward the truck.

I was about to turn away when I saw Lady's head poking out of the bushes. Soaking wet from the storm, she slowly walked out of the field. She kept her distance and remained still, staring at me. I didn't want to startle her by approaching, so I spoke to her. When she heard the sound of my voice saying "Oh my God, there you are!" she knew she was safe again. She wiggled her butt and ran to me, jumped into my arms, and licked my face. I walked around my truck a few times, saying, "She's in my arms. Thank you, Jesus. She's in my arms."

Worried about her health, I drove her directly to the veterinarian. After examining her, the vet was surprised to find that Lady had no visible injuries or broken bones. Amazingly, she had only minor health issues that could easily be treated. Because she had been starving, she had eaten part of a rug and other items, and she had a total of twenty-two ticks on her body. The vet was able to give Lady a clean bill of health, aside from the problems that would heal with time and her return home. He directed me to feed her only small portions a few times a day until her stomach could digest more food.

My grandchildren jumped up and down with joy when they saw me arrive home with Lady. Matthew got on the floor and held her in his arms. For several days, I remained in awe, overwhelmed by this blessed gift.

I decided to inform the public of Lady's awesome miracle by posting another flyer in place of the previous one. It stated that Lady was found safe and was at home, thanks to all the businesses and people who had posted my flyers and allowed them to remain. On this flyer I reminded people to never give up hope. With everything going on in the world, it was refreshing to think of the pleasure of a little town enjoying the happy outcome of teamwork.

For almost three months after her return, Lady stayed close by me. At night she would hide under my bed, something she had never done before. After a few weeks, she stopped that fearful behavior.

One day as it began to rain, I opened the patio door to let her out. She always comes right away when I call her, but this time she must have had a flashback of her ordeal. Her eyes filled with fear, and her ears drooped in terror. Dropping to her belly on the floor, she begged me to let her wait before venturing out onto the patio.

Holding Lady in my arms that day, I thought of the fabled portrait of the Good Shepherd holding his lost sheep. Lady had patiently waited through twenty-eight scary nights, somehow knowing that I would never stop looking for her. Her faith had kept her alive. She had accepted how much she is loved. And she had recognized her master's voice. Whenever I look into Lady's eyes, I am still overwhelmed by the confidence and faith she displayed.

MEDITATION

Lady, Cash, Thumper, Virginia, her family, her friends, and strangers all participated in a spiritual journey that united people to help a lost dog. How has a dog allowed you to experience spiritual growth, or even a miracle, with the support of others?

Life Lessons from Teddy

Diana M. Amadeo, MERRIMACK, NEW HAMPSHIRE

When our third child was about a year old, my husband and I were under pressure to adopt a family dog. During spring break I took the kids to the humane society, where we discovered that none of the pets tugged at our heartstrings. We were halfway out the door when an elderly man arrived with a tiny dog so dirty that it was impossible to determine his color. The man said the dog had been retrieved from the arms of his sister — a hospice patient who had chosen to die in her home. He guessed that the poodle was about a year old.

We asked to see the dog and found him infested with fleas. When the dog played with my kids, he ran around, over, and on them. He jumped up and planted big wet kisses on their lips. Then, tiring of the kids, he suddenly propelled himself onto my chair, licked my cheek, put his head on my shoulder, and fell asleep.

"What is his name?" I whispered.

"Teddy," the old man said quietly. "My sister called him that, but you can change it."

It was an impulse decision — the kids and I debated for only a few minutes. Teddy had become so happy and excited to meet us that he had melted my heart. I worried that if we waited to adopt him, the next person in the door would take him and my children would be disappointed. So I signed papers to adopt the dirty poodle and promised to have him seen as soon as possible by a veterinarian. I had a fleeting concern that there might be more wrong with him than fleas. I wondered if I should slow down and insist that the humane society's vet check him out first. And I worried how my husband would react, since I had failed to include him in this decision. But my overriding concern was that Teddy had just been taken from the arms of his dead owner, whom he obviously loved, and rushed out of familiar surroundings. I didn't want this emotionally fragile being to be caged with dozens of barking dogs.

After we brought Teddy home, I immediately flea-dipped him. To my surprise, he turned out to be snow white.

There was never a question about keeping his name, because it suited him. When we called him Teddy, he immediately reacted with a wagging tail and huge grin. I also felt that Teddy didn't need any more abrupt changes in his life, such as a different name.

Teddy wasn't housebroken, and his behavior was less than desirable. He was by no means a perfect dog. But his imperfection became downright endearing. Whenever he was reprimanded for wetting the floor, his cheerful demeanor — his wagging tail and smiling face — noticeably changed. His tail would drop and he'd hang his head in shame. I couldn't help but grin, forgive, and try to teach him again.

Teddy did not like being alone. There wasn't a cage that could hold him, a door he couldn't open, and a latch that he couldn't figure out. The first time we left him by himself in our home, he leapt onto my son's desk, pulled off the window screen, and tore it to shreds. When we got home, he proudly showed us his handiwork. I found myself wondering how such a little dog could make so profound a mess.

When we had an oak staircase put in our home, Teddy somehow maneuvered around the barricades and left perfect doggie prints in the shiny new coat of polyurethane on the stairs. The next day our carpenter cried out in exasperation, "Teddy, no, no, no!"

As our family grew, we added a second-story porch to our home. The contractor worked steadily for a while and then left the project unfinished while waiting for the windows to arrive. One morning Teddy made his way onto the porch, spied the open cutouts where windows would be placed, and took off at full speed. As in the old Mighty Dog commercial, he soared through ·the air before landing on the ground two floors below. Immediately he began to cry, hold up his paw,

Diana's Teddy

and then limp pathetically. A squirrel gathering acorns caught his eye. In a flash Teddy, suddenly healed, took off to chase the squirrel.

After I had a severe exacerbation of multiple sclerosis, I was left relatively immobile and with visual impairment and hearing loss. Teddy never left my side. He'd lick away my tears of self-pity and place his paw compassionately over my weak hands. Wheelchairs and crutches followed, and Teddy remained by my side, smiling and wagging his tail joyously at my physical progress.

Spasticity can be very painful. Teddy always seemed to know when I was hurting. He would jump on my lap, lay his head on my chest, and give me comfort. His activity level slowed to match mine during my ten-year rehabilitation. We remained inseparable, with him as my shadow.

Teddy could sense my down days, and if I felt weak he would not leave my side. One day I was in the living room, unable to pull myself from the sofa. I was facing our glass front door and watching traffic go by. Normally, Teddy would sit at the glass door and watch the outside activity too, but sensing my weakness he remained leaning against me on the sofa.

A deliveryman brought flowers. He rang the doorbell, and Teddy growled but didn't rush to the door. The deliveryman saw me lying on the sofa, and I motioned him inside. He walked in the unlocked house and handed the flowers to me. Teddy growled at the intruder and climbed on top of me. When the deliveryman left, Teddy jumped off my body and licked my hand, as if to say, "It's okay. I protected you." This tiny nine-pound dog had in his own way ferociously defended me. How could I not smile?

After we'd had Teddy for a decade and a half, his eyes dimmed with cataracts and his hearing progressively worsened. He began having occasional bouts of arthritic pain and developed lateral sclerosis of the spine. When he couldn't make it up the stairs, my husband or children would carry him. About that same time, Teddy started acting confused and he frightened easily. Two years earlier, when he had first shown signs of heart disease, I had talked with the veterinarian about euthanasia. But Teddy had rebounded miraculously, and our life together had continued. Finally, though, despite medications of all sorts, his entire body was simply shutting down, and the time had come to ease his suffering.

The decision — whether or not Teddy should be euthanized — was left to me. I agonized over it, not only because he seemed to rally so often and come back after being close to death, but most of all because I loved him much more than I thought anyone could love an animal. I loved his silliness, clumsiness, kisses, and protectiveness. But I could not leave him in so much pain just because I needed my spirits lifted. When you love someone, you let him go.

I believe that the spirit of a living being never dies. For a week following his death, I could hear the soft clink of Teddy's dog tags, and the familiar sound brought me comfort.

And then I had a dream. Across from me, Teddy sat on a stuffed, black leather lounger. He looked humanlike with his legs crossed. In one paw he held a cigar. In the other paw he clutched a double bourbon. He smiled and said, "I was dying anyway. Don't sweat it." Then he raised his glass in salute and vanished.

This type of dream was totally out of character for me. If, while awake, I had visualized Teddy after death, I would have seen him in the clouds and with wings. But in recalling his antics, I realized that the dream actually *was* Teddy delivering one more of the many life lessons he had taught me. For Teddy wasn't perfect. He was silly. He didn't come off as too smart. He lived life to the fullest, his way. And when his time came, he had no regrets.

Cheers, Teddy!

MEDITATION

The life lessons a dog teaches aren't always lofty or esoteric. Sometimes, they are like Teddy's — live and let live. When has a dog made you smile at the wisdom of his or her ways?

A Familiar Friend Turns Ordinary into Extraordinary

Lori Durante Rardin, BRANDON, FLORIDA

The menacing expression on his face and the fact that he seemed to appear out of nowhere scared me at first. He was just a kid, about twelve or thirteen. But the boy stood taller than my five-foot frame and likely weighed more than I did. He started to walk across the street in my direction.

There wasn't anything unusual about the day I met this young man. I had gone outside around noon as I normally do to play with my Australian shepherd, Piezon. As we walked together along the side of the house to our usual starting point, I heard the dry winter grass crunching under my shoes. The brilliant sun lit up a cobalt blue sky on a perfect seventy-two-degree day in Florida.

The ground rumbled from Piezon's gallop as he raced with an excited bark to catch the ball. He'll do anything to chase a Penn or Wilson tennis ball, in some cases even ignore a treat. This day, his sleek black fur ruffled in the wind. He returned and dropped the ball, waiting for me to throw a second one that I held in my hand.

Without speaking a word, the threatening-looking boy now came directly toward me. He wore a knit cap and had long blond hair protruding beneath it along his neck. His worn denim shorts hung low on the hips, as kids wear them now, but the tail of his long T-shirt covered his back end. I was leery of him, but also annoyed that he was so forward as to approach me. If he were to make an aggressive move, I didn't have a plan of action other than to scream if I needed to.

Piezon fetched the ball at the other end of the yard, and the youngster sat down in the grass a few feet from me. "Who is he? Why does he look so angry? Why is he silent?" I thought. Out loud, I said a simple hello, and he mumbled something unintelligible under his breath. "What's the deal with this kid?" I wondered.

Now that the boy sat cross-legged on the grass near me, Piezon, instead of heading back to me, went straight to him. The dog's embracing brown eyes locked on the teen's face and his slobbery ball slipped from his mouth into the child's lap. Unexpectedly the boy's expression changed. His face lit up at the welcoming invitation from a dog who didn't even know him.

The youngster giggled and threw the ball from a sitting position. Piezon took off at full speed and then returned the ball. His docked tail and entire butt wiggled with wild excitement. The lad stood up to throw the ball harder and farther. Then he finally spoke. "I've had a ba-a-a-d day," he said.

"Oh no, I'm sorry to hear that," I sympathized.

"Today, I lost all of my friends."

Piezon ran back and handed me the ball this time. After throwing it underhand, I said, "Oh, I know how you feel. That's happened to me too." Words spilled out of my mouth without my thinking much about what to say next. "Trust me; I've been around a long time. Things like that happen to everyone. You'll lose friends, get some of them back, and make new friends. Life changes, and so do friends. Things will work out."

My mind flashed back to the old days in middle school with a group of girls I hung out with. We used to go back and forth ousting one friend or another, and I was the one ousted more times than not.

The teenager smiled as the dog approached him again. "Your dog is taking turns giving us the ball."

Lori's Piezon

"But you can throw it farther, and he likes that better."

"How do you get your dog not to run away, since he's not on a leash?"

"Well, by having one of these babies," I said, showing him the extra ball. "It keeps him right by my side."

Piezon's eyes danced with delight. Panting, with his tongue hanging out, my ten-year-old dog slowed his stride on the way back to us.

"What's your name?" I asked.

"Mitchell. I live around the corner."

"Nice to meet you, Mitchell. My name's Lori."

Mitchell giggled as Piezon followed my commands: sit, lie down, roll over.

As Mitchell and I watched the dog perform, I thought about how Piezon had become the greatest experience of my life, other than getting married. My husband and I, unable to have children, had adopted a furry four-legged child instead of the usual two-legged kind. Piezon helped lift us out of a mourning period and into a life with joy-filled puppy activity.

Piezon's name is from the Italian *paesano*, which literally means "countryman." But for our Italian family, *paesano* means more than that. Because your *paesano*s come from the same village as you, they understand your dialect and traditions and treat you as a family member or close friend. So in my family's tradition, *paesano* also connotes "familiar friend." We wanted to give our first dog a unique name while at the same time expressing our need for a familiar friend as we experienced our loss of parenthood. Just as a mother is by the side of her newborn constantly, I made Piezon my constant. He fulfills my natural instinct to nurture.

Piezon's Journey

I decided to tell Mitchell the story of how Piezon came into my life. "When we went to pick out puppies, I wanted a red Australian shepherd, but Piezon picked me!"

"He did?" Mitchell's tone signaled that he was confused as to how a dog picks a human.

"Yup," I answered. "There were two puppies I went to look at to see if I might adopt one. When I arrived at the farm, I was immediately disappointed. Neither of them was red coated. Then I watched as one of the little puppies whined and cried, afraid to leave the mother dog's side. But the other puppy romped around the farm without a care. Not afraid to be away from his mommy at all, the little black and white puffball explored until he got tired out. In his exhaustion, he curled up right in front of my feet and fell asleep. I knew then I wasn't going to get a red Aussie. The other puppy stayed by his mom's side, and Piezon chose me instead to be his mom."

Mitchell listened intently as I continued. "When Piezon was five months old, he landed awkwardly after catching a tennis ball in the air. I heard the crunch of bone. Then he made whalelike, squealing sounds."

"Whoa, poor guy," Mitchell said.

"It was awful. My husband and I rushed him to an emergency veterinary hospital. They took x-rays. His left back leg bone had snapped in half." Mitchell winced as if picturing the broken bone.

"The surgeon placed a pin in Piezon's leg, making it unbendable for six weeks. Another dog might have been hampered by having a pin protruding from his hip. Not my Piezon. He didn't seem bothered by it one bit and effortlessly went wherever he needed to go. He'd look at me with his bright eyes as if to say, 'What's the problem, Mom? C'mon, why can't we play?' "

"I can tell he loves to play," Mitchell said, and threw the ball again. I noticed that my sixty-pound dog was running slower and more sluggishly now. Concerned that Piezon might collapse, I commanded him to lie down while I continued telling Mitchell the dog's story.

"We thought Piezon would never walk properly again. But eighteen months later, he competed in tournaments as a flyball dog." I explained to Mitchell that flyball is a racing game with four dogs on each team. One dog at a time runs a track with hurdles to return a tennis ball. Whichever team crosses the finish line first wins. "Piezon leapt over those hurdles, punched a spring-loaded box to catch the tennis ball, raced back over all the obstacles, and crossed the finish line. Would you have ever known he was injured by looking at him now?"

"No way."

"He's retired now, but he was a master of the game in his prime."

Mitchell then told me about his two Pomeranians and noted that they weren't as obedient as Piezon. He described them and their personality quirks. "I'm going to try to work with my dogs and teach them to obey like Piezon," he said.

"You can do it. All dogs learn if you take time with them."

After talking to Mitchell for an hour, hunger set in, and I said, "Well, Mitchell, I'm going to eat lunch now. Thanks for stopping by. Piezon knew you were sad and wanted to cheer you up. I guess he knew you needed a friend today."

"Yeah, he did make me feel better. Bye."

We went our separate ways, and I felt warm with good cheer because of my dog. Although I had thought at first that Mitchell might be a threat, Piezon's instincts revealed the boy's sadness instead. My dog broke the ice for us, and Mitchell came out of his gloom, if only for an hour.

Piezon's Gifts of Friendship

Just as Piezon did with Mitchell that day, countless times he has lifted me up when I felt low. Somehow he understands my moods and knows when to leave me alone or offer affection.

When he was a puppy, he sometimes tested my limits, but he quickly learned my boundaries. He can get overly anxious when it's time to go for a walk or a ride, but there is still a calmness about him shining through his soulful eyes that makes me feel more serene.

One of Piezon's greatest gifts is his ability to make me laugh. When I do the laundry, his eyes smile up at me and his butt wiggles as if he's asking how he can assist. I purposely drop a dirty sock so he can be my helper by picking it up and handing it to me.

Piezon not only gives his friendship to humans but also befriends other animals. I remember the time I took in a frightened young stray dog so I could help her find a home. Her rescuer had named her Blaze because of her fiery brindle colors. She was comfortable around dogs but petrified of people. Whenever a new person came into Blaze's space, she'd cower. But Piezon greeted people with happy smiles and wiggles. Blaze would study Piezon's fearlessness and carefully come over to sniff the person. His positive example showed the insecure dog how to be confident. The pup came out of her shell and had grown into a happy, well-adjusted dog by the time a new family adopted her.

On the day I met Mitchell, as he has many other times, Piezon
lived up to his name. He is my familiar friend who makes ordinary
days into extraordinary days.

MEDITATION

It's easy for humans to misjudge or prejudge people based
on external cues. Has a dog ever revealed someone's true
character to you?

I'll Have Hunny with My Sake,
Thank You Very Much!

Diane L. Massie, BALDWINSVILLE, NEW YORK

This story begins with an ending — the events that led up to the passing of my beloved shih tzu–poodle mix named Sake. But Sake's exit from my life was actually the next step in what has been an ongoing and most extraordinary journey of the heart. Throughout our thirteen years together, little Sake and I danced around each other in an emotional ballet of wills. Our daily pas de deux? What I call the *tension tango.* As in the tango dance, my rigid and inconsistent attempts at warmth and love would send Sake signals of acceptance one moment and rejection the next. This little black and white, curly-tailed guy wanted only to be loved but was left in a constant state of emotional insecurity.

Our confusing emotional war was apparent at our very first meeting. As I tried to choose between Sake and his docile little puppy sister, he promptly asserted himself by peeing on me. Misinterpreting this act as a sign of independence and character, my response to his challenge was: "Well, I guess that's it, then. I'll take this one!" It turned out to be a prophetic moment. Throughout the ensuing years, everyone has been quick to reiterate: "And he's been peeing on you ever since." Ha, ha, people; very funny.

Journeying home to begin our domestic relationship, I thought about what to name the little dog I'd adopted. The Far Eastern origin of the shih tzu breed, combined with his seemingly drunken antics as he sought to maintain balance in his crate in the moving car (okay, no driving comments), brought to mind the rice wine called sake. And so Sake became his name. Warning: names have power. Sake frequently displayed the erratic behaviors and unpredictable responses associated with the overindulgence of wine. I would often see him lying relaxed on the sofa and then watch him suddenly go ripping through the house at warp speed. Or snuggling with his stuffed toys one moment and tearing them to shreds the next.

In our version of a domestic relationship, Sake and I were a snarky little dog and a rigid, anxiety-ridden perfectionist. We were best described as curmudgeon times two. Having invited

Diane's Sake

Sake into my world of work, work, and, well, more work, I would allow him to enter only on my controlling, type-A terms (we will walk now; we will play now; we will huggy-snuggy now). Sake, however, came into my life with his own plan, clever boy. Whatever emotions I expressed, he faithfully mirrored right back to me. If I was cranky, he'd be snarly. If I was impatient, he'd be demanding. To my mind, this was a power war: guardian versus dog, leader versus follower, controlled versus uncontrolled. Sake's view? Woman being an idiot versus dog giving a flawless portrayal of a Tasmanian devil. And so our tension tango continued.

On we went, year after year, coexisting in what gradually became comfortable conflict. Then, as happens in war, we were wounded — I, with a chronic illness; he, with blindness and general ill health. Suddenly neither of us had control over any-thing, and we were scared. We cried together, snuggled together, and faced painful medical procedures together. We spent so much time at the local animal clinic that I used to ask my veterinarian which one of his kids went to college on the Sake scholarship.

Eventually Sake was referred to specialists at the Cornell University Hospital for Animals. It was a long drive there, and our many visits provided Sake and me with a lot of quality time in the car. He'd lie in the passenger seat as I rubbed his tummy and ears with one hand and drove with the other. Often he'd stretch across the seat and fall asleep snuggled against my arm, and we would drive in companionable silence. During one of these trips I was overcome when I suddenly realized that Sake and I were no longer simply comfortable; we were *comforting*. This amazing insight opened my heart that day. Parked at Cornell, I remained in the car as I strove to understand and assimilate this powerful release of emotions. I felt elation and lightness. My entire being relaxed. The inner war between Sake and me came to an end as I realized that, all along, I had really only been at war with myself.

Sake, mirroring my emotions as always, climbed into my seat then, licked away my tears, and snuggled in my lap. At this moment, an unconditional love rushed through me that overwhelmed the inflexible, the judgmental, and the fearful in me, and it broke the barriers I had long ago set up to keep others at a distance. Little Sake had set me free. And just like that, he went from being Mr. Snarly to being my little sweetie, tootsie-pie, Hunny Bunny. Our old issues disappeared. We became Team Unconditional Love.

Sadly, several years later, it became my responsibility to set Sake free from his pain. But you know what? He had taught me well. For through the tears, the loss, and the loneliness, my heart stayed open to love and to being loved.

I'm Not Ready

Repeatedly after Sake's passing, I announced to my friends: "I'm not ready for another dog. I'll wait a year or so before even thinking about it." Unconvinced, my friends, God, and the spirit of Little Sake, I'm sure, initiated a propaganda program. Every day, someone or something would present me with the message that I should get a dog.

The craft fair I attended turned out to be a sponsor for greyhound adoptions. Portions of the proceeds went to the local greyhound rescue chapter, which had several dogs in need of good homes. Colleagues at work all knew someone who was giving away a dog. New billboards advertising dog-related items and events sprouted up along my daily travel routes. A dear friend came to visit, and, as it happened, she wanted to stop at the local animal shelter on our way back from shopping. This bombardment continued for weeks, and I took to shouting "Incoming!" to signal each new dog-related incident, providing a chuckle for those around me.

I finally surrendered to the inevitable after I returned home from a brief visit to Canada. I found my phone answering machine crammed with messages, all from the same friend, about a dog. *Beep:* "You really should call this number." *Beep:* "At least speak to this woman," my friend pleaded. *Beep:* "I feel really positive about this." ARGH! After about the fifth message I caved and called the number.

As it turned out, the woman I spoke with at that number was involved in small-dog rescue and made it her job to keep track of little dogs available in local shelters and pounds. Totally ignoring my firm pronouncement that I was "really not interested in a dog at this time," she proceeded through her list. There were two old Lhasa apsos whose human had been displaced. The woman wanted someone to take both of them. There was an aged shih tzu (Oh no, too much like Sake!), and a Chihuahua mix who was slated to be euthanized in a few days. "But I'm really not interested in a dog at this time?" I whined with a question mark at the end of the sentence.

"Well," she continued, "you could at least call or go and see the Chihuahua. Perhaps if someone shows interest, they'll hold off euthanizing her for a while."

"Okay," I thought, "this woman's good. She's really good." Knowing I'd been completely bested and guilted, I said, "All right, I'll call the shelter."

A good-deed trip to the pound on a beautiful August evening truly was no imposition, so I went to visit the little dog. The pound turned out to be a veterinary office–kennel that served as the holding area for dogs picked up in the city. They generally kept stray dogs for two weeks before euthanizing them. However, this little

Diane's Hunny Bunny

Chihuahua mix was so sweet that the kennel employees had lobbied for her daily and managed to hold on to her for an additional week. The day I arrived to see the dog was Thursday. On Monday her time would be up.

The kennel door opened. In trotted a dog who gave the term *mixed breed* new meaning. She was like a Mr. Potato Head for dogs, looking as though parts of different breeds had been randomly stuck together to create her. She had huge ears like a kangaroo, a small head, and a beagle tail. Super skinny and with patches of fur missing due to a flea allergy, she was a shaking, quaking, scared little dog. When the receptionist asked, "Well, what do you think of her?" I found myself unable to decide whether to label her "appealing" or "appalling" and opted for responding, "Well, she leaves me speechless."

I sat down and waited and waited for the dog to approach me. Finally, curiosity got the best of her, and she jumped up onto my bench. Side by side, we listened as the attendants related the brief history of how this dog had been found running loose on the street in a not-so-desirable part of town. They had no idea how long she'd been lost. She had no collar, microchip, or other identification of any kind. I was the only person who had even made an inquiry about her.

Visiting time ended. As the veterinary worker picked up the dog to take her back to the kennel, I casually asked, "What have you been calling her?"

"She likes to burrow under a blanket and hide all the time," the attendant replied, "so we've been calling her Bunny."

It was as if an electric shock zapped into the top of my head, through my body, and into the earth. They called her Bunny, and Bunny had been part of my favorite nickname for little Sake. Something cosmic was definitely going on here. Dazed and with mumbled thanks, I hurried out to my car. Filled with shock, awe, and gratitude, I burst into tears.

On the drive home I had an epiphany. I couldn't ignore the fact that the entire process that had led me to Bunny had been one of complete synchronicity. I acknowledged I was lonely, and that living alone with a chronic illness was a struggle. I remembered how I'd prayed that my next dog would be a gentle, loving, huggly-snuggly little soul. So, what to do, what to do? God had sent me what I'd asked for, but this was way too soon. Not my time line, uh-uh, not ready. But, oh no, what if this was a one-time-only offer?

After arriving home, I immediately phoned the kennel. "I'll take her," I proclaimed. "Can I pick her up tomorrow?" I made arrangements to adopt Bunny amid sounds of cheering and clapping by the attendants.

The next day, someone told me that immediately after I called, a couple came into the kennel and said they would take her. No one had wanted Bunny for three weeks, and suddenly two opportunities had appeared. Clearly, this little dog was meant to be saved, and I was fortunate enough to be first on her list.

Remember what I said about names having power? Well, my little Hunny Bunny is the sweetest, most loving and lovable dog friend. We play together, snuggle together, and leave singing messages on friends' phone machines together. Our joy in the relationship uplifts each of us.

Do we have issues? Sure. The trauma she experienced while living on the street still lingers. She runs for cover at any sudden noise and hates going outside. Little bunny nests made of dog blankets that she burrows underneath lie scattered throughout the house.

On my side, chronic illness is exactly that, and takes a daily emotional toll. Our blessing is that we nurture each other's hearts despite our circumstances. Hunny Bunny truly is, as I like to say, "love in a dog suit."

I thank you, dear little Sake, and your friends in high places for guiding me along the path to love.

MEDITATION

Have you had the experience of feeling that one dog led you to another? Why and how do you think this happens?

Finding a Keeper Named Cissy

Mary Haack, ARVADA, COLORADO

A little white paw timidly poked through the bars on the cage. Looking down to find out what was attached to this little paw, I saw a white foxlike face with a big smile and huge mahogany eyes. The dog wagged her tail as fast as she could. She had almost no hair, and her belly was still distended from recently birthing pups.

I knelt down, holding the little paw, and was rewarded with kisses from this beautiful dog. She looked to be no more than a puppy herself. "American Eskimo — Female," read the tag over the cage at Denver Municipal Animal Shelter. Her age was estimated at one year, and she needed a loving home. "Ken," I called out to my husband, who was a few cages away, "I think I found a keeper."

My recently widowed mom was looking for a companion to fill her lonely nights. Her daytime hours were tolerable, but the long evenings and nights without my dad had left her feeling alone and even more despondent. We thought a small, loving dog would bring her comfort. She'd asked for an older dog who didn't have to be housebroken and would lie on her lap or at her feet at night while she watched television.

Ken brought Mom over to the American Eskimo's cage, and the dog was ecstatic to have so many people paying attention to her. She did two little circles, bowed, and tapped her front paws on the floor of the cage. Then she rubbed sideways against the gate, so we would pet her. Mom took an immediate liking to the dog. Ken and I were relieved. We had been visiting shelters in the Denver area for weeks now, and Mom hadn't seen any dogs she cared for.

I wondered if it was my imagination, but this pup seemed to have eyes only for me. I was surprised at myself for thinking that way. After all, the dog was for Mom. I had no interest in adding a dog to my already busy life of working full-time, parenting a teenager, and being Mom's support system. And yet it wasn't only me who noticed. "The dog acts like she wants to be Mary's more than mine," Mom said. My heart dropped. I did my best to act nonchalant. "She's happy, Mom, with a lot of love to share, and she's just what you need."

We discovered then that the little white dog had given birth to a litter of puppies shortly before being picked up while wandering the streets of Denver. The shelter staff had no idea where the pups were. In the two weeks since she'd arrived, no one had come forward to claim this lovely, nearly hairless dog. Spaying her was an absolute must, and then she would be available for adoption two days later. The staff assured Mom that the dog's hair would eventually grow back. They explained that it was normal for this breed to drop its fur during the final stages of pregnancy and while birthing pups.

After she had been spayed, Ken picked up the dog from the clinic. Because she was still woozy from the effects of the anesthesia, Ken carried her into Mom's house. The dog's sleepy eyes found mine immediately, and her tail gave a small wag. Ken put her in my lap, and she fell asleep with a soft sigh.

While gently petting her, we tossed around ideas for her new name. Since she was white, we went through names like Cotton, Snowball, Snowie, Cloud — all the obvious ones. Then Mom told us that as a child she had had a puppy named Cissy, whom she adored. The dog was hit by a car, and Mom had been devastated.

Even though we chuckled and said it was a rather "sissy" name, our family duly approved it. Because I happen to think all living creatures deserve a middle name, I tacked Ann onto the name Cissy. My Mom was a devout Catholic, and at confirmation ceremonies people of that faith often add the names of patron saints to their birth names. To take this naming process a step further, and to tease my mom, I chose the additional name Marie because it went well with Ann. The family laughed at what we could now call "Mom's Catholic dog." Even Cissy woke up long enough to wag her tail at the happiness and laughter she had already created. Now Cissy Ann Marie had a new home, and Mom had a new companion.

Life with Cissy Ann Marie Wasn't Heavenly

Unfortunately, this new relationship wasn't made in heaven after all. Mom wasn't as ready for a dog as she thought. Cissy kept escaping through the front door. She peed on the floor. She chewed up tissues, climbed on the furniture, and generally turned out to be more work than Mom had expected. After two short weeks Mom announced that she was giving poor little Cissy back to the shelter.

We were distraught at the news. Mom maintained that she was simply too old to chase after a rambunctious puppy. My husband and daughter wanted to keep Cissy and train her properly. I felt torn, not only because taking on the responsibility of a dog is a lot of work, but also because we had recently lost our elderly beagle. Molly Brown was a sweet little dog who had wandered into our backyard one day and ended up staying. We'd had her for years when her hearing and vision began to diminish, as happens with older dogs. Our new house had a swimming pool, and, unfortunately, one day Molly fell in the pool and drowned. It was a tragic accident and difficult for us to recover from. We never knew if she'd had a seizure and fell in or cut a corner during her walk along the deck. Molly Brown's accident made me wonder if we even deserved another dog.

Taking up my usual pondering position, I sat on the kitchen floor to consider all possibilities. Cissy quietly climbed into my lap, gave my chin a couple of kisses, and settled in while softly sighing. I was hooked. There was no way I could allow this wonderful dog to be returned to the shelter. We told Mom that we would care for Cissy, train her, and then give her back when she knew how to behave for a senior citizen. Once it was made, I felt good about the decision. Sure, this would be more work for me, but I had a hunch Cissy would be worth it, and her love overpowered any apprehension I might have had. Besides that, I thought, training Cissy shouldn't take too long. In no time at all, Mom would have an obedient, loyal dog.

For the rest of that spring and into early summer, Cissy managed to terrorize our house and backyard too. She pulled the cover off of our pool and chewed it, along with the pool hoses and spa cover. She chewed the corners off her doghouse and anything left on the floor. Then she would cuddle up to us, her large brown eyes begging for understanding but still full of joy and mischief.

We registered Cissy for dog training classes. She played, barked, pulled at her leash, sniffed everything in the room, and kept smiling with delight. We were certain she would flunk puppy class, given her reputation as the class clown. The all-important device of giving treats to train a dog didn't do a thing for her; she ignored them and did whatever she wanted.

One day she spontaneously reacted to a hand signal for the stay command, and we praised her verbally with excitement in our voices. Cissy looked at us with pure pleasure and proceeded to complete the course while we continued to offer only verbal praise, not treats, as positive reinforcement. She graduated and from that day forward was an extremely obedient dog, always willing to please. Although Mom began to comment on what a good dog Cissy was turning into, we said nothing about returning her. Cissy had wormed her way into my heart and filled a void I hadn't even known I had. However, our success with Cissy would soon pave the way for Mom's own happiness with a dog.

Cissy's New Mission

One cold February morning a few years ago, I awoke with a horrible headache, extreme vertigo, a thick tongue, a foggy mind, and numbness on the left side of my face. These symptoms continued for weeks. Doctor after doctor failed to find an answer to my problem. With Cissy by my side, I would lie in bed with the curtains drawn and the doors closed to keep out noise. I slept and cried while my dear pup licked tears off my cheeks as fast as they ran down.

Mary's Cissy

When my husband entered the dark, gloomy room, Cissy would let out a small growl and move even closer to me until he spoke gently and assured her that he had no intention of harming me. When I could walk, she followed and wouldn't even let me go into the bathroom alone. She began going to doctor appointments with me and attending my physical therapy sessions. Because Cissy became upset when people touched me, I did the sessions each time in a room where there were no other patients and always with the same gentle therapist that Cissy had learned to trust.

I had frequent panic attacks and stuttered uncontrollably without Cissy nearby. But when she was with me, and I had physical contact with her, I was able to talk to strangers. It became apparent that I could speak relatively well when the attention was not on me. With people focusing on my dog, I didn't feel that others were judging me, and so I could simply talk about my favorite subject, Cissy. Incredibly, she instinctively knew when I was about to have a panic attack. She would guide me away from the source of my anxiety, whether it was noise or a crowd of people, or climb into my lap and lean gently against me.

I was finally diagnosed with multiple cranial neuritis. For the rest of my life I would have migraines, vertigo, memory problems, and panic attacks. This meant I needed to learn to live with my condition. After observing Cissy and me together, one of my doctors wrote a prescription making Cissy my official service dog. Now, with Cissy's assistance, I could begin to venture into society.

As it turns out, having Cissy is one of the main reasons I've been able to move on with my life. Her comforting ways have reduced my stress levels. I acquire a gentle strength from her when I rest my hand on her soft fur. Similar to the little pink blanket I had as a child, Cissy provides me with a feeling of security that has been sorely lacking since my illness began.

Expanding Cissy's Service

One day when I was at our local library, I saw a brochure for the Exempla Lutheran Medical Center Pet Therapy program. I just knew that Cissy would be great at animal-assisted therapy. I made a little promise that, if I could be on my own for a few hours at a time, I would share the love of my angel dog with other sick people. After all, Cissy was the reason I had progressed so well with my recovery.

I was enthusiastic about the program and really wanted to participate in it, but the brochure sat on top of my dresser for about two weeks before I gathered enough courage to call the number listed on it for more information. Wrestling with my own self-doubts, I kept asking myself if the hospital would be willing to take on and train a person with disabilities, even though I have a dog with so much love to share.

On the day I called the pet therapy program number, I spoke to the volunteer services coordinator, Debbie, who was so very nice. She made it easy for me to explain my situation and convey my desire to be a pet therapy volunteer. Debbie assured me that the volunteer trainers would be delighted to work with me. She talked about the qualities they were looking for in a pet therapy team and explained that the teams were carefully screened to satisfy the hospital's liability insurance requirements.

I began to feel apprehensive because of my social anxieties and was anxious about making this big step. Would I remember everything? Would people like us? The most obedient dog still has a mind of her own — would I be able to make sure that Cissy followed all the rules? Since barking and licking were at the top of the list of no-nos, I wondered if I could stop Cissy from barking when she was happy or from kissing people when she felt they needed it. As I mulled over my decision, Cissy's gentle, confident eyes reassured me. Wordlessly, she conveyed to me that we could do this together, as a team.

The volunteers in the pet therapy program were wonderfully caring with me, and they adored Cissy. The three leaders of the program helped us with every step in the application and training process. It usually takes about four months for a dog and handler to be trained for pet therapy. It took us a lot longer, but we were diligent, and I wanted desperately to volunteer. My various disabilities had left me with feelings of inadequacy — I needed this chance to give back to the community and to prove my worth.

I was trained in hospital codes, procedures, and protocol. Cissy had to pass two screenings by at least two volunteer veterinarians, who assessed her health and emotional and physical abilities. She took various tests that judged her reaction to loud noises, slamming doors, having her ears and tail pulled, and encountering equipment such as wheelchairs and IV poles — anything she could possibly experience in a hospital environment. Pet therapy dogs must remain calm and not nip, bark, or overreact to situations.

On our first therapy visit, a volunteer trainer shadowed us. I ended up having a panic attack, but Cissy was marvelous. She passed with flying colors, and the patients loved her. My next supervised visit went more smoothly. As long as I petted Cissy, I was able to knock on doors and enter patient rooms and converse with the occupants, mostly about Cissy. One woman wanted to see Cissy close up, but I didn't have the physical strength to hold my dog over the bed. As if she knew what we wanted, Cissy jumped up on the visitor's chair. I pushed the chair over to the bed so that the patient could pet and love Cissy. We were becoming good at creative teamwork. From that point on, when we visited the hospital, Cissy jumped up on every chair she was allowed on so that the patient could gain access to her soft, silky fur.

The leaders of the pet therapy program are thrilled with our progress. They marvel at how well Cissy shares her love with sick people and the stressed-out medical staff. Nurses and doctors love the therapy dogs as much as the patients do.

As soon as I take the purple uniforms that we wear for pet therapy out of the closet, Cissy becomes animated because she knows she is going to work for a couple of hours. As she enters the hospital, her tail curves tightly over her back, and she holds her head high. She is ready to perform her duty. When we leave the hospital, we are exhausted, and naps are in order for both of us. Cissy and I are extremely proud of our joint effort to give back to the community and help people deal with sickness.

Cissy Stays Home

Because of the incredible bond that Cissy and I have and Mom's loving acceptance, we never did give her back. Mom ended up adopting an American Eskimo dog of her own, whom she named Missy. She enjoyed her for many years, and after Mom passed away, Missy, by then thirteen years of age, came to live with us. Missy is losing her eyesight, and Cissy walks with her, side by side, fur to fur, directing the blind dog wherever she needs to go. Even though Cissy sometimes steals Missy's food, they are the best of friends.

Last summer Cissy developed a reaction to one of her vaccinations, and we almost lost her. Suddenly our roles were reversed as I spent every second by her side, taking care of her and loving her and praying for her recovery. She had begun bleeding internally, and to save her life she was given immediate blood transfusions. Even in her weakened state, with all she had to endure, her eyes still sought me out. Her flowing tail struggled to wave back and forth and showed me she was fighting to stay alive. It took a full year for her to return to good health.

Due to her weakened condition, Cissy had to take a leave of absence from pet therapy. We are now back to work on a part-time basis working in what are called "special units." This consists of Cissy and me visiting larger groups of patients and their families in the chemotherapy infusion, outpatient surgery, and medical imaging areas. We don't have to walk as far and are able to sit down while visiting.

Cissy will soon be on another leave of absence because the back left part of her body is not working well. I have been giving her supplements, prescriptions, hot baths, and acupuncture and will explore doggie chiropractic. I am hoping things will get right with her again soon.

I just know that, from heaven, Mom had a hand in Cissy's earlier miraculous recovery. From the beginning, Mom always knew that Cissy was attached to me. As she watched our relationship grow, she saw that I loved Cissy with all my heart and instinctively must have known that Cissy and I would need each other to survive.

MEDITATION

Cissy seemed to know intuitively that becoming a therapy dog would bring joy to both her and Mary. What have similarly inspired dogs shown you about new directions in life?

Winning the Love of a Dog
Who Wouldn't Kiss Me

Linda Anderson, MINNEAPOLIS, MINNESOTA

He refused to kiss me. No matter how many times I kissed him, he would not return the affection. Kind of reminded me of a book that was popular around the time he came into my life. "He's just not that into me," I thought about this dog we had rescued.

Unlike every dog I'd ever had, this guy was, first of all, male. All my previous canine companions had been females who showered me with warm, sloppy kisses from day one. But not this little black cocker spaniel with the bright ebony-colored eyes, the turned-up nose, and the frantic expression on his face. He looked as if his world had crazily spun out of control. And so it had.

Only a few months before we met the dog who wouldn't kiss me, our beautiful yellow Labrador retriever, Taylor, had died. Both my husband, Allen, and I were devastated. Our house with only cats, Speedy and Cuddles, and our cockatiel, Sunshine, had become unnervingly quiet. Cats tread softly, their paws gently gliding along the surfaces of a home. The bird, except for his occasional song, chirp, or screech when someone was at the door, silently observed the world from his high cage. As odd as it may seem, we missed noise.

No metal dog-collar tags chimed. While I cooked meals in the kitchen, I heard no sounds of Taylor slurping water from the dog bowl with her long, pink tongue. There was no heavy padding of her paws climbing up and down the stairs, keeping vigil between my office and Allen's.

After we lost Taylor, I continued to do necessary tasks associated with the books that Allen and I write about animals. All the while, I grieved in the sad stillness of mourning for the seventy-pound dog who used to sprawl across my foot while I worked. I always joked that if Taylor could have had one wish, she would have asked not to be our dog but to serve as our skin. Some folks call animals like her "Velcro dogs." Taylor could never get close enough.

I loved how, when I stretched out on the living room couch to relax after a long day's work, she'd lay her body atop mine. Draping her front paws over my shoulders, she'd rest her head against my chest and listen to my heart beating.

Dogless

After Taylor was gone I entered a period when I needed her more than ever. She had nurtured me through my breast cancer and knew how to help me cope with the most stressful of times. Before and after her death, Allen and I were writing a book about animal rescue that focused heavily on the aftermath of Hurricane Katrina. Thousands of animals had perished, and thousands more were rescued by dedicated volunteers and organizations. Our publisher had the book on a fast track for release on the one-year anniversary of the hurricane.

The anxiety of meeting nearly impossible deadlines, interviewing hundreds of people for the book, and hearing searing stories of loss and devastation had taken an emotional toll on me. Then we were into interviews and presentations and book signings, where I relived stories of suffering followed by healing and, in some cases, happy reunions of people and lost pets. I sorely missed my doggie heart-monitor, Taylor, after spending long days revisiting painful memories that left me exhausted.

Taylor was no longer available to take the long lakeside walks that relieved my stress and renewed my energy. It had been three months since she stood still next to Lake Calhoun one June day, looked at us with pleading eyes, and lay down on the ground as if to say, "I can't take another step."

As our busy days flew by without the pleasure of Taylor's company, we began to realize that we could no longer stand living in a home without a dog. The cats too were grieving the loss of their lumbering buddy. They had raised her from puppyhood to respect their species and claws. They had appreciated that our house was safer with Taylor's deep, rumbling bark to ward off danger. Lately Cuddles and Speedy had started popping images into my mind to say that they were cats, after all, and could only protect us up to a point. What we needed was a dog. What we all needed was for Taylor to come back home. But that wasn't going to happen. Going dogless didn't suit any of us.

The Carpet Comes Alive

Although we hadn't planned on adopting a new dog so soon, there Allen and I were, on a cool autumn day, with our car magically pointing us toward our local animal shelter. Just to take a look.

After arriving at what we couldn't admit was our destination, we walked through the rows of kennels where dogs of many breeds and colors took various stances for or against relating to the human species that had betrayed them. Some pressed their faces against cage doors and stared longingly at us. Others hovered timidly in corners, trembling. Still others turned their backs and ignored humans, who, based on their experience, were untrustworthy at best, abusive and neglectful at worst.

We asked the volunteer who accompanied us if we could take

a couple of the dogs out back for a walk. The first one, a terrier mix, seemed bonded with the volunteer and only had eyes for her, even after the volunteer stepped out of the dog run. The second, a Lab mix, glared at us and refused to play with the ball we threw for her to retrieve. Nothing clicked. No dog crooned to us with the soul song that said, "You were meant for me."

I searched the shelter again, in case there might be some dog who called to my heart. Out of the corner of my eye, I saw a thick, black patch of carpet rolled up on a kennel floor and felt the nudge to take a closer look.

As we headed out the door, past the cage that had caught my eye, the rolled-up carpet came alive. A head popped up off the floor. Four little legs, which had been stretched out front and back, lifted the dog's black body up from the concrete. A pair of dark, deep eyes with an expression of wanton longing transfixed me. "Could we take a look at that little cocker spaniel before we leave?" I asked the volunteer. "Sure," she said, "you can see Harley."

The cage door clanged open after the volunteer removed its metal lock. She wrapped a blue leash that looked like a lasso around the dog's neck and brought him to us. The dog skittered forward, tugging her along with nervous energy, heading for whatever freedom he imagined outside his prison cell.

As the volunteer and Allen walked the dog toward a private room where we could visit, I stopped to read the sign posted on the dog's cage door. It listed his breed, size (twenty-five pounds), and coloring. In the section labeled "Reason for relinquishment" there was only one word: "Abandoned."

After the volunteer left Harley and us to get acquainted, we sat on a tiled bench in a private room and waited to see what the dog's next move would be. At first, his eyes registered fear at being alone with strangers. Then he jumped up, put his paws on my knees, and looked into my eyes as if he were inspecting me. This was unusual — most dogs don't make such blatant eye contact.

A family with young children walked by the room and Harley forgot about me, showing much more interest in the little kids. I said, "Maybe he needs a home with children." All this time, Allen had been sitting stiffly on the bench, making no move toward the dog. He explained later that he was still grieving so much over Taylor that he felt as if he would be disloyal to even consider loving another dog.

Probably sensing that he might be about to lose his chance at escape, Harley stopped trying to get the children's attention and returned to give me another once-over. I squatted on the floor, intending to play with him. He rolled over in a submissive move, and I rubbed his belly. Feeling his silky, curly fur slip through my fingers after so many months of not touching a dog made me euphoric. I said to Allen, "Come and pet him." Reluctantly Allen stroked Harley's back and scratched behind his ears. I wondered if he needed this wiggly bundle as much as, if not more than, I did.

Well, we're adults, right? We should make sober, considered decisions and not be as impulsive as kids chasing after an ice cream truck. To convince ourselves that we needed to think through this major decision, we turned to the volunteer when she returned for Harley and said in our most mature-sounding voices, "We should go home and think about this."

And she said, "He's a purebred cocker spaniel. He could be gone by the time you decide. Do you want to put a twenty-four-hour hold on him?"

That seemed a reasonable, rational thing for two responsible people to do. She took Harley back to his cage. We went to the checkout counter to take care of the paperwork.

Consulting the Cats

On our way to the parking lot, we agreed that we'd done the right thing. After all, we had to go home and talk this over with the cats and the bird. A new family member would affect them too. We'd sleep on it and decide in the morning.

All the way home, our conversation centered on Harley. "Do you think he'd want his own water bowl instead of Taylor's? That is, of course, *if* we adopt him. It's still an 'if,' isn't it?"

"Where will he sleep? We'll have to get a dog bed."

"He's much smaller than Taylor, so we should buy a new collar and leash."

"We gave away the rest of Taylor's dog food. We'll need to buy more."

While Allen drove, I pondered whether it might be a good thing that this black cocker spaniel was not big and would be a dramatic departure from the much larger yellow Lab and golden retriever we'd had during our marriage. Taylor had *loved* me but *adored* Allen. As fond as I was of her, I'd secretly longed to someday have an affectionate smaller dog who might focus on me.

With all our recent work writing and promoting the animal rescue book, I had felt a desire bubbling inside me to rescue our next dog. So many animals, even purebred dogs, are available at shelters and through breed-rescue groups. And they desperately need people to restore their confidence in humans and give them love and safety. Maybe Harley would be both my small, cuddly dog and an animal who forever showed me gratitude for having rescued him.

Upon arriving home from the animal shelter, we brought the cats into the living room, where the bird watched the proceedings from the perch in his cage. We told them all about Harley. They listened intently. Later, an animal communicator had a conversation with them and learned that as we talked about the possibility of a new dog, the cats had envisioned their amiable friend Taylor, not a cat-chasing cocker spaniel who would terrorize them.

Sensing (or thinking wishfully) that our pet family had given its blessing to the new dog, Allen said, "He looked so lonely in that big cage."

"How can we leave him in the shelter one more night? What time do you think they close?" I asked.

"We could take him to the pet supply store and buy essentials. He'd be settled in here before morning," Allen replied.

I made a list of all the items we'd need, while Allen drove us back to the animal shelter.

Bringing Baby Home

With only about a half hour until closing, we hurried to the animal shelter's checkout counter. A volunteer pulled up Harley's papers and read the sparse information about him to us.

"The video camera recorded a man and woman on a Harley-Davidson motorcycle leaving him and another dog in the after-hours drop-off area at our other facility. The staff named him Harley because of the motorcycle. A veterinarian checked him over and did the operation to neuter him. Harley has an ear infection. We'll give you medications. When he wasn't adopted in the first week, the staff at the other shelter thought he'd have a better chance if they sent him here, where we get more visitors."

I waited for Allen to sign the papers. And then I felt it — a waterfall of unearthly, warm, white light beamed through the top of my head and into my body all the way down to my toes. The love contained within this light was almost unbearable. I clutched the counter, trying to steady myself. Instinctively I knew that this dog, this soul, had at that moment entered my life and united with me. At a deeply spiritual level, my family and I would welcome this tiny being of light into our pack.

Another volunteer brought Harley out to where we waited for him in the lobby. Harley pulled on the leash, surging through the door like a racehorse onto the track. He literally couldn't wait to get out of that place.

We took Harley to the grassy lawn outside the shelter, and I sat on the edge of a stone embankment while Allen walked him. A woman stopped and complimented us on how cute a dog he was. She had treats in her pocket and spontaneously taught our new son to sit by lifting her hand and holding a reward above his head. When he instantly plopped his little rear end down on the grass and opened his mouth for the treat, she said, "This is a smart dog." I beamed with pleasure. A smart, cute dog. What more could we ask?

Because the dog had so much scattered energy, we decided it would be best to exercise him around our favorite lake, where we used to walk Taylor. On the drive to the park, a Harley-Davidson approached in the next lane and idled beside our car at the stoplight. The motorcycle's namesake lurched forward from the backseat where he'd been looking out the window and inserted himself between our two seats. He firmly planted his front paws on the middle armrest, glared at the motorcycle, and growled with a deep, low rumble. "I don't think he wants to be called Harley," I said to Allen.

But what would be his name?

When we arrived at the park, we started to walk; we were careful not to call him by the name of the machine that he obviously found reprehensible. Autumn leaves raked into piles dotted the sidewalks along the trail. Red, gold, and brown leaves drifted earthbound. Our new dog went wild with glee. He hurled his body into the leaf piles and rolled around in them. He looked up, fascinated, at windblown leaves floating aimlessly from nearly barren tree branches. His name settled into my mind as softly as the fallen leaves landing on the ground. "I think he wants to be called Leaf," I told Allen.

Reality

The first night home with Leaf was a nightmare. He didn't want to sleep in the crate we'd bought for him at the pet store. He didn't want to sleep on the soft pillow of his dog bed. He didn't want to sleep at all, which meant we were awake most of the night with him.

The first month home with Leaf was a disaster. He seemed to have never experienced the inside of a house. Our carpet took the place of grass as his potty. Our terrified cats were transformed into his favorite prey. Every unexpected sound in our home prompted his fearful howling and whimpering.

If we merely walked out of the room where he sat or slept, he howled with such piteous intensity that our neighbors must have thought we were beating him. He'd fall asleep and wake up dazed, wailing and whimpering with his eyes rolled back, not knowing where he was and clearly having a flashback of being left to fend for himself. Soon we realized that we had rescued an unhouse-broken dog with post-traumatic stress disorder and hellish separation anxiety. As far as we could tell, he'd never had a toy or any kind of human affection. He remained frightened, aloof, and scattered no matter how much we tried to reassure him that he was safe.

An animal communicator talked with Leaf and told us that he

may have been a puppy mill dog. His breed is so popular that un-scrupulous people have overbred and sold unhealthy dogs to an unsuspecting public, mostly through pet stores. Leaf had the char-acteristics of a dog who had experienced very little human con-tact and was kept outdoors. Fortunately, other than having a delicate digestive system, he didn't suffer the terri-ble physical health issues these miserable creatures usually have. That was a good thing, since he had a nearly rabid response to even the mildest veterinary care.

Linda's Leaf

When I caught inner glimpses of Leaf's past, I saw him living the life of an outdoor dog along with the companion who had been left with him at the shelter. His previous humans may have purchased him at a pet store — cute little cocker — but appar-ently hadn't had the patience or interest to housetrain him. Then they left him on the side of the road. A kindly couple on their Harley picked up the two dogs and drove them to the after-hours entrance of the animal shelter. At least, that's the story line I re-ceived when I tuned in to the memories Leaf was willing to share with me.

All of Leaf's issues overwhelmed us at times, but we believed that with patience, and by enrolling him in doggie school, we'd find ways to help him heal. I missed Taylor even more now that Leaf, with his extreme fears and needs, had taken over our lives.

I'd pet him, and he'd allow it. But if I leaned down to kiss his head, he offered no affection in return. Oh, how I longed for one more of Taylor's sweet doggie kisses.

Wish Fulfillment

I don't remember the exact date that it happened. A couple of months after Leaf became a member of our family, I bent down to kiss him on the forehead between his eyes. He raised his head and examined my face carefully, as he had on our first visit at the animal shelter. Then with his raspy pink tongue, he planted a big, wet kiss, not on my mouth, but on my nose.

One kiss. I thought I would die of happiness.

From that point on, our kissing sessions burgeoned from one to two to three or four carefully placed nose licks. By Christmas, I was the thrilled recipient of kisses in the morning, kisses in the evening, and definitely kisses at his suppertime.

It's now been five years since we adopted Leaf. He no longer chases the cats. They return the favor by tolerating his presence. He rarely has accidents in the house. If he does, it's usually our fault for being so focused on work that we don't pick up his signals, or a symptom of his having eaten something he shouldn't. He loves to play with Allen, whom I call "Leaf's favorite toy."

He responds to all kinds of commands that aren't in the typical dog obedience playbook (such as "Go get Daddy") and understands words we had no idea could be in a dog's vocabulary (such as *popcorn*). He's a happy, well-adjusted family dog with dog and human friends at dog parks, our favorite doggie daycare, and our ever-patient groomer's office. He greets invited visitors at our house with gusto. His muscular body, and his ability to spring from his back legs as if he were plunging through the front room picture window, make our house safe from intruders. Even the cats must appreciate that about him. When we arrive home, his stubby tail wags in rapid circles and he makes us feel like returning royalty.

We enjoy long walks with Leaf around the neighborhood and the lakes and feel the tensions of the day diminish with every step. He makes me laugh out loud at least once a day and always brings a smile to my face. Although he still wants affection on his own terms and in his own time, he cuddles with me on the sofa, places his paw across my knee, and claims me for his own.

About six months ago, Leaf started a new bedtime ritual. He jumps up on our bed, paws at Allen's side, pulls down the covers, and assiduously prepares it for his favorite playmate's arrival. Then he rolls over on his back while I rub his tummy. I ask, "How was your day?" He vocalizes by moaning and moving his mouth, trying to say words that will tell me about his visit to the dog park, our walk around the lake, or the fact that Allen took him to the pet supply store — whatever constitutes the highlights of a pampered cocker spaniel's existence.

After I'm tucked in, with my head propped up on pillows and a book in my hand to read, he sits at my shoulder and gazes lovingly and intensely into my eyes. His nighttime kissing centers on my nose, which he carefully and methodically, up and down and sideways, licks for as much as a minute. Satisfied that he's settled me in for the night, he says goodnight to Allen with a lick or two. I get many more kisses, I guess, because Leaf knows I need them. He rests his head on my shoulder and falls asleep while I read. He stays there until I turn off the light. At that point, he jumps off the bed and goes back to sleep either on his adjacent dog bed or in the bedroom doorway — ever protective, ever watchful. I fall asleep listening to his gentle sighs, snores, and snorts.

I've been kissed by many dogs in my life. No kisses have been sweeter than Leaf's. Maybe it's because I had to earn them. Maybe it's because he decided that he was ready to express gratitude and love for the gift of our relationship. Maybe it's because we love each other, and that's what you do with the one you love — you kiss her on the nose.

MEDITATION

What are your experiences with a dog's kisses? As you fall asleep tonight, remember them, and you're sure to have sweet dreams.

Afterword

The sage sees the One in all beings....
In a Brahmana endued with wisdom and humility,
in a cow, in an elephant, as also in a dog...,
the wise see the same.

— *The Bhagavad Gita with Commentary by Sri Sankaracharya*

Few other relationships in this world ever match the sincerity, devotion, and joy that exist between a woman and her dog. When she gazes into the eyes of a creature who trembles with unconditional love and unbridled happiness at the very sight of her, she is glad to be home. Her dog makes a woman get physical exercise, entices her to play, sparks her interest in life from a canine's point of view, and ensures that she is needed and appreciated. If she feels low, the warmth of dog's fur rubbing against her skin, or the exuberance of a tail-wagging greeting, lifts her spirits. If life is going well, who is better at joining in the celebration than her loyal companion? Sensing her moods, her dog adapts to them and unreservedly gives whatever support is necessary.

During the period of time when a beloved dog enriches her life, a woman has the benefit of a best friend, a gentle listener, a canine therapist, an energetic playmate, a loyal protector, and an accurate judge of people's characters or intentions. Soul to soul, women and dogs bond at a spiritual level that transcends creeds and belief systems. At the end of her dog's life, the woman's searing pain of loss is indescribable to any who have not experienced its intensity. And yet, her memories, her dreams, and the spiritual experiences she has after the dog's death remind a woman that love lives on long after the physical body is gone.

In the pages of this book, you have met dogs who inspired people to give selfless service. These dogs have also helped their humans to forge bonds of family and friendship with each other. You have made the acquaintance of incredible dogs and amazing women who saved each other's lives. In some cases, the lifesaving has been physical; always it has been emotional and spiritual, with the partnership lifting each partner to greater levels of fulfillment.

Our hope is that this book will raise the bar when it comes to viewing dogs and other animals as family members. These stories reveal the vital roles that dogs fill in a person's home and in inspiring a woman's destiny. The next time you bend down to pet a furry head or scratch behind a floppy set of ears, consider how dogs inspire you to become a better, kinder, more gracious human being. Then tell the world, or at least your corner of it, that each dog is special; each dog is important; each dog, when offered the opportunity, is masterful at giving and receiving love.

Listen to your heart when you consider adopting or fostering a rescued dog or forming a lasting relationship with a canine companion. You will join in a sisterhood of women that has lasted throughout the ages. Your sisters and mothers have looked at dogs sleeping by their sides or curled up on their laps and silently whispered, "You are my heart." The dogs have stirred, wiggled, felt the ecstasy of a woman's freely given love, and wordlessly responded, "I adore you."

Acknowledgments

With respect and love, we give our appreciation to Georgia Hughes, New World Library's editorial director, who has worked with and encouraged us to bring to the world the messages in *Dogs and the Women Who Love Them*.

We are grateful to the wonderful visionary Marc Allen; the marketing director and associate publisher Munro Magruder; our enthusiastic and amazing publicity director, Monique Muhlenkamp; managing editor Kristen Cashman; type designer Tona Pearce Myers; cover designer Tracy Cunningham; editor Bonita Hurd; proofreader Karen Stough; editorial assistant Jonathan Wichmann; and all the staff at New World Library.

We sincerely appreciate the encouragement from Harold and Joan Klemp, who inspired us on our journey of giving service by writing books about the animal-human spiritual bond.

Our deep gratitude goes to Rory Freedman for writing this book's foreword. Her book *Skinny Bitch* inspired us and millions of others to embrace a lifestyle that reduces cruelty to animals by making more mindful and healthier food choices.

A special thanks to all the incredible women who shared stories in this book about their cherished experiences and profound friendships with dogs.

We greatly appreciate the wisdom and generosity of judges for the 2009 Dogs and the Women Who Love Them True Story Contest: Darlene Arden, Connie Bowen, Keith Miller, Patrycia Miller, and Marcia Pruett Wilson. The contest became the rich resource for most of the stories in this book.

We extend our heartfelt gratitude to Stephanie Kip Rostan of Levine Greenberg Literary Agency, Inc., our energetic literary agent.

We also thank members of the Saturday Morning Minnesota Screenwriter Workshop sessions led by Chris Velasco for all the support and affection. The Loft Literary Center continues to be a beacon and haven for writers, and we are grateful for our relationship with this outstanding organization.

Our families instilled a love of animals in us at an early age. We especially appreciate Allen's mother, Bobbie Anderson, and Linda's mother, Gertrude Jackson. To our son and daughter, Mun Anderson and Susan Anderson: you're the best. Much love to Allen's sister, Gale Fipps, and brother, Richard Anderson, and their families.

Special thanks to Darby Davis, editor of *Awareness* magazine, for publishing our column, "Pet Corner," all these years, and to Kathy DeSantis and Sally Rosenthal for writing consistently beautiful book reviews. To Lessandra MacHamer: you have always been in our corner, and we love you for it.

And thanks to our current animal editors, Leaf, Speedy, Cuddles, and Sunshine. Without you, we wouldn't have been able to fulfill our purpose.

Notes

Introduction

Epigraph: Jalal al-Din Rumi, "The Turn: Dance in Your Blood," in *The Essential Rumi*, translated by Coleman Barks with John Moyne, A. J. Arberry, and Reynold Nicholson (New York: HarperSanFrancisco, 1995), p. 279.

1. Jon Franklin, *The Wolf in the Parlor: The Eternal Connection between Humans and Dogs* (New York: Henry Holt, 2009), pp. 258, 216, 254.
2. Ibid., p. 254.
3. Ibid., p. 258.
4. Ibid., p. 216.
5. Ibid., pp. 214–15.
6. Carl Zimmer, "The Secrets Inside Your Dog's Mind," *Time*, September 21, 2009, www.time.com/time/magazine/article/0,9171,1921614,00.html (accessed December 12, 2009).
7. "Man's Best Friend Actually Woman's Best Friend; Survey Reveals That Females Have Stronger Affinity for Their Pets Than Their Partners," *Business Wire*, March 30, 2005, http://findarticles.com/p/articles/mi_m0EIN/is_2005_March_30/ai_n13489499/ (accessed December 31, 2009).
8. Michael J. Silverstein, Kate Sayre, and John Butman, *Women Want More: How to Capture Your Share of the World's Largest, Fastest-Growing*

Market (New York: HarperBusiness, 2009), as quoted in "The Family Pet Ranks Higher Than Sex to These Women," *USA Today*, August 25, 2009, http://content.usatoday.com/communities/pawprintpost/post/2009/08/having-a-pet-ranks-higher-than-having-sex-to-these-women/1 (accessed September 9, 2009).

9. Jon Franklin, *Wolf in the Parlor*, p. 160.

One. Loyalty

Epigraph: Janice A. Farringer, "Comfort Zone," in *Dog Blessings: Poems, Prose, and Prayers Celebrating Our Relationship with Dogs*, edited by June Cotner (Novato, CA: New World Library, 2008), p. 44. Published with permission of the author. All rights reserved. Janice A. Farringer is a poet and writer living in Chapel Hill, North Carolina. She welcomes comments at jafarringer@gmail.com.

Two. Healing

Epigraph: Bernard S. Siegel, MD, "Dogs as Spiritual Messengers," in *The Lazy Dog's Guide to Enlightenment* by Andrea Hurst and Beth Wilson (Novato, CA: New World Library, 2007), p. 9. Published with permission of New World Library. All rights reserved.

1. Patriot PAWS Service Dogs, "Archie, Patriot PAWS Service Dog, Named Dog of the Year," www.patriotpaws.org/newsroom.html.

Three. Embracing Life

Epigraph: Josephine Preston Peabody, "To a Dog," in *The Best Loved Poems of the American People*, edited by Hazel Felleman (New York: Doubleday, 1936), 582–83.

1. Thomas Moore, *Soul Mates: Honoring the Mysteries of Love and Relationship* (New York: HarperCollins, 1994), p. xvii.

Afterword

Epigraph: *The Bhagavad Gita with Commentary by Sri Sankaracharya*, translated from the original Sanskrit into English by Alladi Mahadeva Sastry (Madras, India: Samata Books, Copyright by V. Sadanand, 1987), p. 171.

Contributors

One. Loyalty

SALLY ROSENTHAL, "More Than a Guide Dog." A former college librarian and occupational therapist, Sally Rosenthal is the book reviewer for *Best Friends Magazine* and Disabilityresources.org. A contributing editor to *laJoie*, she and Greta, along with her husband, Sandy, and his service dog, Pumpkin, are pet therapy and hospice volunteers. Organizations Sally mentions in her story are Guiding Eyes for the Blind, www.guidingeyes.org; Pals for Life, www.palsforlife.org; and Puppies Behind Bars, www.puppiesbehindbars.com.

MARILYN WALTON, "K-9 Major — from Chains to Heroism." Marilyn Walton is a graduate of Ohio State University. She has written six children's books, which were published by Raintree Steck-Vaughn from 1983 to 1986, and she authored *Rhapsody in Junk: A Daughter's Return to Germany to Finish Her Father's Story* (AuthorHouse, 2007). Marilyn is the author of *Badge on My Collar: A Chronicle of Courageous Canines* (AuthorHouse, 2007) and its sequel, *Badge on My Collar II: To Serve with Honor* (AuthorHouse, 2009). She is a member of the Eighth Air Force Historical Society and conducts research on World War II. She and her husband raised three sons in Oxford, Ohio.

JANET BALLARD, "K-9 Major — from Chains to Heroism." Janet Ballard attended the University of Montevallo and the U.S. Army Military Police Academy. She is an award-winning, nationally recognized K-9 trainer and handler and member of the U.S. Police Canine Association. She is a four-time winner of the USPCA National Field Trials and head trainer at Caliber Kennels in Chandler, Arizona, where she and her husband make their home. She currently commutes between Arizona and Minneapolis, where she trains detector dogs for the Minneapolis–Saint Paul International Airport.

TERESA AMBORD, "A Working Girl Turned Our Senior Center into a Family." Teresa Ambord lives in far northern California and works from home as a full-time business writer for BizActions.com. For fun, she writes stories about her family and her small posse of dogs. She also serves as a foster parent for abused and abandoned animals through Another Chance Animal Welfare League (www.anotherchanceanimal welfareleague.org).

ROSANNE NORDSTROM, "Miguel's Legacy." Rosanne Nordstrom lives in Chicago with her husband, Roger, and their two cats. When she's not spending time with Paco's daughter, Princess, she writes and practices the violin. Paco is always in her thoughts, and she's happy whenever she sees him.

SUSAN HARTZLER, "Growing Up Dog Weird." Susan Hartzler is up-to-date on the latest trends for dogs. She and her current pack, Baldwin and Bliss, have their own iPhone publication, *DIY Doggie*, and their own webstore, Alpha Dog Shopper (www.alphadogshopper.com), where they review products. Baldwin and Bliss are pet therapy dogs at Los Angeles County–USC Medical Center and Children of the Night (www.children ofthenight.org). They live happily with their feline sister, Cyd Cat the Contessa de Calico, and their thirty-year-old cockatiel brother, Boy George.

KAREN DAWN, "Remembering Buster Dawn." Karen Dawn is an author and radio host who has written for the *Los Angeles Times* and *Washington Post* and who founded the animal advocacy media watch website DawnWatch.com. Her first book, *Thanking the Monkey: Rethinking the Way We Treat Animals* (HarperCollins, 2008), was chosen by the *Washington Post* as one of the best books of 2008. You'll find a video of Buster Dawn's greatest hits on Karen's blog at ThankingtheMonkey.com.

Two. Healing

LORI STEVENS, "Lori and Beau Say to Disabled Veterans: 'You've Got a Friend.'" Lori Stevens is a certified pet dog trainer with twenty years of experience. She holds a provisional membership in Assistance Dogs International. Lori has been employed by and has volunteered for several dog-training organizations, including Lone Star Assistance Dog Service and Texas Hearing and Service Dogs. In August 2009 the American Legion Auxiliary presented Lori with its Woman of the Year award. Lori founded the nonprofit Patriot PAWS organization (www.patriotpaws.org) in February 2006 and continues as its president. Patriot PAWS trains service dogs to perform various behaviors, including supporting patients with post-traumatic stress disorder. The organization's primary goal is to increase the self-sufficiency of people with disabilities. Patriot PAWS has a continuing commitment to match disabled veterans with dogs and to assist the vets and dogs in learning to work together as teams. After writing her story for this book as a tribute to Beau, Lori was saddened by his passing on March 14, 2010, three days shy of his fifteenth birthday.

JENNY PAVLOVIC, "My Journey with 8 State Hurricane Kate." Jenny Pavlovic, a writer, speaker, blogger, animal rescuer, and biomedical engineer, lives in Minnesota with her three dogs, Bandit, Chase, and Cayenne. She wrote the true story of Kate's remarkable journey in the award-winning book *8 State Hurricane Kate: The Journey and Legacy of a Katrina Cattle Dog* (8 State Kate Press, 2008). Fifty percent of the book's profits go to Kate's legacy, the 8 State Kate Fund, providing financial relief for animals in desperate situations. Learn more at www.8StateKate.net. Jenny's second book, *The Not without My Dog Resource & Record Book* (8 State Kate Press, 2010), includes essential information about dogs in a user-friendly format for daily use, travel, and emergencies.

SAGE LEWIS, "The Rescued Dog Who Became My Buddha Boom!" Sage Lewis, Creature Teacher, has a slogan she lives by: "Helping pets and people become happier, healthier, and better behaved." Her work with animals and people includes Tellington TTouch, animal communication, behavior consulting, end-of-life consulting for pets, shamanic healing, coaching for pets, and life coaching for people. She has hosted *The Pet Playground* radio show and is the author of *Java: The True Story of a*

Shelter Dog Who Rescued a Woman (Greenlight, 2006). Visit her website at www.DancingPorcupine.com.

KIM DUDEK, "Dagnabit and Kim, a New Orleans Love Story." Kim Dudek is the founder, owner, and president of the award-winning Belladonna Day Spa in New Orleans, which provides a beautiful environment, luscious products, relaxing services, and a well-trained staff. Belladonna has become a focal point in the community and has done fund-raising and charitable giving for such causes as tsunami victims in Thailand, the New Orleans Jazz Orchestra, the Susan G. Komen Foundation, and the New Orleans LA/SPCA. Kim is the founder of the nonprofit organization Dag's House (www.dagshouse.com), where she and her staff specialize in the shelter, fitness, and rehabilitation of special needs dogs. Kim personally now has six dogs. Dag's wheelchair was made by Doggon Wheels (www.doggonwheels.com). In March 2010, Dag was named Pet of the Week in the e-newsletter of the Humane Society of the United States, and Dag's photo by Skip Bolen won the organization's 2010 Spay Day Online Pet Photo Contest.

BOBBI LEDER, "Euri, the Miracle Worker." Bobbi Leder has been published in a variety of print and web magazines, including *Dog Living Magazine, Tails, Pet Talk, Urban Paws,* and *Texas Cats & Dogs Magazine.* She is the Houston Dogs Examiner, writing a weekly online dog column for the Examiner website, in which she spotlights dogs who need homes. She also writes for a local print publication, *The Banner.* Visit her website at www.bobbileder.webs.com.

BARBARA TECHEL, "The Blessing of a Wheelchair-Bound Dachshund." Barbara Techel is the award-winning author of the true, inspirational book series *Frankie, the Walk 'N Roll Dog.* Learn more about her and Frankie on their website (www.joyfulpaws.com) or on Facebook (at www.facebook.com/joyfulpaws). To follow along on Frankie's adventures, check out Barbara's blog at www.frankiethewalknrolldog.blogspot.com. To reach the two organizations mentioned in Barbara's story, go to Therapy Dogs Inc., www.therapydogs.com, and Eddie's Wheels, www.eddies wheels.com.

LINDA PANCZNER, "Better with Barney." A lifelong reader of others' words, Linda Panczner is finding out what it's like to be the creator of text. After testing out various genres, she has found that writing about animals seems natural, since it is easy to tap into her deep, sincere passion about her own experiences with a menagerie of meaningful pets.

DEBRA J. WHITE, "For Two Dollars She Was Mine." Debra J. White is a freelance writer, retired pet therapist, and animal shelter volunteer. She also volunteers with the Sierra Club and the Department of Economic Security for the state of Arizona. She lives in Tempe with four rescued dogs.

JILL ALLPHIN, "The World's Best Talking Dog." Jill Allphin lives in Corvallis, Oregon, with her husband, Terry, and Calamity Jane, their talking cat. She works for the Department of Human Services, is a member of the Oregon Writers Colony, and has had stories published in *Seasoned with Words* (Oregon Writers Colony, 1998), *A Cup of Comfort Cookbook* (Adams Media Corporation, 2002), and *The Spirit of Corvallis* (Donning Company, 2008).

Three. Embracing Life

JUDY MCFADDEN, "Judy and McDuff: Soul Mates on a Spiritual Mission." Author Judy McFadden writes about her nine years with McDuff, the mystical, stubborn, and hilarious Scottish terrier therapy dog. She lives in Henderson, Nevada. Visit www.lifewithmcduff.com to order *Life with McDuff: Lessons Learned from a Therapy Dog* (Summit Mountain, 2009) and learn more about Judy and McDuff. Excerpts of this story were first published in *Life with McDuff: Lessons Learned from a Therapy Dog* and are used with permission of Summit Mountain Publishing. Opportunity Village, with its Project PRIDE, mentioned in Judy's story, is at www.opportunityvillage.com.

VIRGINIA CONSIGLIO, "Lady, the Miracle Dog." Virginia Consiglio is a Fair Haven, Michigan, resident blessed with three children: Matthew, Theresa, and Michael. Virginia has a history of volunteering. As chairperson of the beautification commission located in Harrison Township, Michigan, Virginia spearheaded and orchestrated breaking ground, construction, and the dedication and opening ceremony for the Harrison Township Veterans Living Memorial. She also has great compassion for the boxer breed of dog, which led her to contribute her time and efforts to foster rescued boxers with two organizations, Wigglebuttz and Mid-Michigan Boxer Rescue, which have merged (see www.mid michiganboxerrescue.org). She enjoys target shooting and renovating her home. Currently she is pursuing her profession as a licensed Realtor, which has kept her busy for the past fourteen years. Her website is www.therealty executive.com. She welcomes emails at therealtyexecutive@comcast.net.

DIANA M. AMADEO, "Life Lessons from Teddy." Award-winning author Diana M. Amadeo sports a bit of pride in having 450 publications with her byline in books, anthologies, magazines, and newspapers. Yet she humbly, persistently, tweaks and rewrites her thousand or so rejections with eternal hope that they may yet see the light of day. She can be reached at DA.author@comcast.net.

LORI DURANTE RARDIN, "A Familiar Friend Turns Ordinary into Extra-ordinary." Lori Durante Rardin's uplifting stories have appeared in magazines such as *Angels on Earth*. Her book for women struggling with infertility is titled *This Too Shall Pass: A Handbook for the Emotions of Infertility* (Chasing Rainbows, 1999). Linda welcomes contact at Ldr411@aim.com. Visit her tributes to Piezon, who has passed away since Lori wrote this story, at http://petsupports.com/a05/piezon01.htm, and http://petsupports.com/a05/piezon02.htm.

DIANE L. MASSIE, "I'll Have Hunny with My Sake, Thank You Very Much!" Diane L. Massie recently retired from a career as a professional musician and teacher. She is currently pursuing her passion for writing and study-ing gemology and enjoys being able to spend more time with Hunny Bunny. She is a strong advocate of the benefits pets bring to the chronically ill. Diane and Hunny Bunny welcome email at dmassie@twcny.rr.com.

MARY HAACK, "Finding a Keeper Named Cissy." Prior to Mary Haack's ill-ness, she worked as an office administrator. She now writes as a form of therapy — something she can do from her home at her own pace. She has had several short stories published in local newspapers and has volunteered at the local senior center, teaching beginning writing classes. Due to Cissy's popularity with the patients and staff at Exempla Lutheran Medical Center, Mary has set up a web page for Cissy at www.mycissy.com.

Additional Photographers

Except for the following, the photographs accompanying the stories in this book were taken by the contributors.

Page x: Photograph by Diana Mrazikova, www.dianamrazikova.com. Copyright © Diana Mrazikova. All rights reserved.

Page 6: Photograph by Skip Franz, www.skipfranz.com. Copyright © Skip Franz. All rights reserved.

Page 61: Photograph by Monty Marsh, courtesy of www.guerillafilm worx.com. Copyright © Monty Marsh. All rights reserved.

Page 98: Photograph by Allen Brown, Eden Prairie, Minnesota, www.Allen BrownPhotography.com. Copyright © Allen Brown. All rights reserved.

Page 111: Photograph by Skip Bolen, www.skipbolen.com, www.skip bolenstudio.com. Copyright © Skip Bolen. All rights reserved.

Page 172: Photograph by Susan DeWulf for Michelle Nikiforuk, Bark-A-Bout Pet Resort, Shelby Township, Michigan, www.barkabout.net/. Copyright © Bark-A-Bout Pet Resort. All rights reserved.

About Allen and Linda Anderson

Allen and Linda Anderson are inspirational speakers and authors of a series of books about the physical, emotional, and spiritual benefits of having pets as family members. In 1996 they cofounded the Angel Animals Network (where pets are family) to share stories that convey uplifting messages about the relationships between people and animals.

In 2004, Allen and Linda Anderson were recipients of a Certificate of Commendation in recognition of their contributions as authors in the state of Minnesota.

In 2007, their book *Rescued: Saving Animals from Disaster* won the American Society of Journalists and Authors Outstanding Book Award.

The Andersons' work has been featured on the *Today* show, *ABC Nightly News*, *The Montel Williams Show*, and the Animal Planet network, as well as in national wire service articles, magazines, and newspapers, including *USA Today*, the *Washington Post*,

Best Friends Magazine, Dog Fancy, Cat Fancy, and *Animal Wellness*, among others.

Allen Anderson is a writer and photographer. He was profiled in Jackie Waldman's *The Courage to Give*, a book that was featured on *Oprah*. Linda Anderson is an award-winning playwright as well as a screenwriter and fiction writer. She is the author of *35 Golden Keys to Who You Are & Why You're Here*. Allen and Linda teach writing at the Loft Literary Center in Minneapolis, where Linda was awarded the Anderson Residency for Outstanding Loft Teachers.

The Andersons share their home with a dog, two cats, and a cockatiel. They do fund-raisers for animal rescue organizations and donate a portion of revenue from their projects to animal shelters and animal welfare.

You are welcome to visit www.angelanimals.net, Allen and Linda's website, and their homepages and groups on Facebook (search "Linda-Allen Anderson" and "Angel Animals") and Beliefnet (Angel Pets Fan Club). They invite you to send them stories and letters about your experiences with animals. At the Angel Animals website or by email, you may also request a subscription to their free email newsletter, *Angel Animals Story of the Week*, which features inspiring stories about animals around the world.

Contact Allen and Linda Anderson at:
Angel Animals Network
P.O. Box 26354
Minneapolis, MN 55426
Websites: www.angelanimals.net and
www.dogsandthewomenwholovethem.com
Email: angelanimals@aol.com

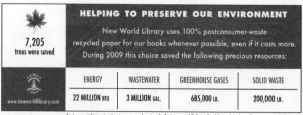

HELPING TO PRESERVE OUR ENVIRONMENT

7,205 trees were saved

New World Library uses 100% postconsumer-waste recycled paper for our books whenever possible, even if it costs more. During 2009 this choice saved the following precious resources:

ENERGY	WASTEWATER	GREENHOUSE GASES	SOLID WASTE
22 MILLION BTU	3 MILLION GAL.	685,000 LB.	200,000 LB.

Environmental impact estimates were made using the Environmental Defense Fund Paper Calculator © www.papercalculator.org.